DJ & Molly,
Long time Friends!

How to Prevent, Detect, Treat, and Live with

The Addict Among Us

by Bradley V. DeHaven

With a foreword by Congresswoman Mary Bono Mack

Dedication

To all of the parents I have met and those who I have not met who have lost a child to drug overdose or addiction.

Table of Contents

Index of Tables and Figures

Acknowledgments

I have been so inspired by parents—like Jodi Barber who lost her son Jarrod to an overdose and had the courage to not only make the documentary "Overtaken" but to march into every school she could, demand their attention and work to educate teens about addiction; and the Rubin family who push their quadriplegic son Aaron's wheelchair in front of teen audiences so that they may see the ramifications of drug abuse. Also by Avi Israel, who honors the memory of his son, Michael, through his tireless efforts to institute prescription drug reform with his organization, Save the Michaels.

Special thanks to Natalie Costa and Brent Huff for allowing me to be a part of the documentary "Behind The Orange Curtain," a remarkable film that will raise awareness of this epidemic. Thank you to all of the hardworking staff of addiction treatment centers for their dedicated efforts to take our addict from us and hand us back our loved one. Thanks to Alan Baker, for his assistance with statistical research. Thank you to my Editor, Robin Martin of Two Songbirds Press for her complete dedication to this project.

Thank you to my partner in life, my rock—my wife Lisa, for believing in me and supporting me in following a passion that was born inside me in our most difficult times. I thank my son Bryce for his support and understanding during the most uncertain times and helping me with my business as I follow my passion. Thank you to my son Brandon for allowing me to tell our story in hopes of saving others our fate and worse. Thank you Brandon for having the will and the power to return to us, rejoining our family when we often thought we would never see you again.

A special thank you to Congresswoman Mary Bono Mack. I am awed by your honesty as you advocate alongside grieving parents for awareness, education and reform. Thank you for honoring me by writing the Foreword for *The Addict Among Us*.

Foreword

As many Americans have learned all too painfully, "the addict among us" often times is a son or daughter, mother or father, best friend or next door neighbor. But quickly, their heartache becomes our heartache...their sorrow, our sorrow...their journey, our journey. Sometimes, if we're very lucky or really paying attention, we can spot the addict right away; other times we simply have our lingering, nagging suspicions; but all too often, we are totally and utterly clueless until we're knee deep in a life-or-death struggle. Here's the sad truth: The addict among us is everywhere. In this compelling and provocative new book, Brad DeHaven finally shines a light into the darkness of addiction, and the jagged abyss that swallows tens of thousands of families a year.

As Americans, we rally around efforts to fight breast cancer, childhood diseases and other serious health threats. But for far too long, there have only been hushed whispers about prescription drug abuse—now the fastest growing drug problem in America, according to the Centers for Disease Control and Prevention—and, in many ways, the new definition for self-destruction.

So as the death toll from prescription drug overdoses continues to rise dramatically, it's time to move this story from the obituary page to the front page where it belongs. But first, we must resist the soul-soothing temptation offered to us by denial, and ignore the door that leads to the easy way out. Because in the end, "see no evil, hear no evil" often leads to a society's unspoken evil—the tragedy and travesty of indifference.

As a nation, it's time to realize that we can't simply wish this horrific problem away. Not with more than 20,000 people a year dying from it. Not when the number of babies born addicted to the class of drugs that includes prescription painkillers has tripled in the past decade. Not when nearly one out of four high school seniors have used prescription painkillers.

Simply put, prescription drug abuse is more than a public health epidemic—it's a national tragedy.

As Chairman of the U.S. House Subcommittee on Commerce, Manufacturing and Trade, I have held several nationally-televised hearings on this devastating and rapidly-escalating problem. As Honorary Chairman of Mothers Against Prescription Drug Abuse (MAPDA), I have witnessed first-hand how pervasive this scourge is in our neighborhoods, communities and schools. And as a child—and later in life as a wife and mother—I have actually lived and loved—and struggled and survived—with "the addict among us."

In many ways, my family is like so many others all across America. We have suffered through the heartbreak of addiction; we have celebrated the life-changing moments of remission; and we have encouraged each other to remain ever vigilant and always mindful that the path of recovery can be winding, bumpy, and never-ending. The substances of choice for my loved ones ranged from alcohol to prescription painkillers, but the devastation caused by their abuse is the same.

When I first shared publically what my own family was going through, so many wonderful people in turn offered their own stories, and vowed to help in the fight against this debilitating and often-times deadly disease. And while addiction touches each family in very different and personal ways, tens of thousands of Americans today are going through something similar. Together, we need to join forces to dramatically raise awareness of this epidemic and create a nation dedicated to preventing, treating, and recovering from substance abuse and addiction. But time is not on our side: Prescription drug abuse is getting worse every single day, and a comprehensive national strategy for combating it is desperately needed.

Think about it. If 20,000 people died each year from food poisoning, Americans would demand immediate action—or else. Washington bureaucrats would be scrambling for solutions; Congress would rush to pass new laws; and the national media would be investigating the reasons for the crisis. So why has it taken so long for our governmental agencies to get serious about combating prescription drug abuse? The Food and Drug Administration's Risk Evaluation and Mitigation Strategy (REMS) for Extended-Release and Long-Acting Opioids is a classic example of a plodding agency muddling its way through piles of indisputable evidence.

Can anyone explain why the FDA took more than three years before deciding recently that drug companies which make "extended-release or long-acting painkillers" must provide expanded education to prescribers and consumers about the dangers and risks of addiction? How many people died needlessly in the meantime? Instead of three years, it should have taken the FDA about three minutes to take action after looking at the skyrocketing statistics and horror stories all across America. But the FDA isn't alone in the blame. The DEA, NIDA, SAMHSA and even Congress have all been slow to react.

So what's the answer? I believe one critically important first step is to do a better job of monitoring and limiting access to prescription painkillers such as OxyContin, Opana and Vicodin. The next step is to make certain that doctors, dentists, nurse practitioners and other prescribers are up to speed on the dangers of addiction. Otherwise, the consequences can be deadly.

Last year, a desperate addict walked into the Haven Drugs Pharmacy in Medford, New York, and murdered four people for 11,000 tablets of hydrocodone—an opioid used to manufacture a long list of narcotic pain killers, including Vicodin.

One of those gunned down was a customer, thirty three-year-old Jamie Taccetta, who was engaged to be married. Instead, she was buried in her wedding dress. A pharmacy employee, seventeen-year-old Jennifer Mejia, was also killed and later buried in her prom dress along with her high school diploma.

It was an absolutely senseless tragedy, and the latest and most horrific example of a growing wave of drug store robberies by prescription drug addicts. But it's also part of a larger, rapidly-escalating struggle nationwide against prescription drug abuse and addiction.

Why is it happening? Scientists tell us that childhood trauma, genetics, mental disorders, depression, stress, anxiety, thrill seeking, peer pressure, severe pain from injuries and illnesses and even the horrors of combat all contribute to prescription drug addictions, which can lead to tragic and avoidable deaths.

But what's even more insidious is the way these powerfully addictive narcotic prescription drugs quickly turn people without any real emotional or physical problems into desperate people suddenly facing life-or-death struggles. Few things are more destructive personally or harmful to our communities. Recently, I met in California with dozens of parents who have lost their children to prescription drug abuse. Two classes of medicines—painkillers and insomnia/anxiety drugs—are responsible for about 70 deaths and nearly 3,000 emergency room visits a day. That's right—a day. These are truly stunning numbers, but they also just scratch the surface of the problem.

According to the Centers for Disease Control, drug overdose is the leading cause of accidental death in the United States, surpassing automobile accidents for the first time—in large part due to prescription drug abuse. And the problem is growing. An estimated 7 million people age 12 or older regularly abuse prescription drugs, and there are approximately 7,000 new abusers every day—many of them teenagers and young adults. This alarming trend is taking a huge, unmistakable toll on our society.

For people all across America, prescription drug abuse is a day-to-day struggle. Over time, it can destroy families and wreak havoc on communities. Someone with a toothache or a sore back should not be prescribed a potentially addictive painkiller. Clearly, expanded public education plays a role in addressing this problem, but we're not going to make any real progress until we limit access to these powerful narcotic drugs and ensure that only patients in severe pain can obtain them. Today, I have legislation pending in Congress to accomplish this goal.

The pervasiveness of prescription drug abuse made national headlines when federal, state and local law enforcement agencies, led by the Drug Enforcement Administration, cracked down on so-called "pill mills" in Florida, resulting in dozens of arrests—including many doctors.

Congress needs to make it much more difficult for these rogue pain clinics to operate, and we should treat offenders like any other street drug dealer. By better coordinating the efforts of local, state, and national agencies—and by reducing the supply of highly addictive opioid painkillers—I am convinced that we can eventually save thousands of lives and spare millions of American families from the heartache of addiction.

No child should ever be buried in a prom dress again because America ignored "the addict among us." After reading this book, you'll better understand what's at stake for our nation and our society.

~Mary Bono Mack

Introduction

Sixty first and second-year high school students sit on black plastic chairs in the media center for their Health class on a Friday morning. They are the usual mix of students of a variety of races and attitudes: the group of boys in black hoodies, the giggling girls with hairbrushes at the ready, a pair of big dudes with lettermen jackets, a girl with a long side braid texting on a pink cell phone, a loner with her nose in a book, one guy in a cowboy hat who immediately puts his head down on the desk. I am here during the unit on drug abuse, of course, and I suspect the kids are pretty incredulous.

Today's group is pretty quiet; after all, it is just before 8 a.m. when I start talking. I'm an old guy, another lecturer warning of the dangers of drugs. They appear underwhelmed as another presentation on just say no to drugs prepares to start their day. Let the blah...blah...begin. I tell them how I did a drug bust to keep my son out of prison. This gets the attention of some. After a while, I show them a video of my eldest, who is now in his mid twenties, detoxing from Oxycontin on our bathroom floor when he was twenty two-years old. This grabs the attention of them all, though I must insist that the kid with his head down put his head up for this video. I have no proof, but suspect he may need to see it more than the others.

Ten students in this group (one in six) admit to knowing someone who has tried someone else's prescription; but national statistics put the number at one in five, and Placer County's much higher as are many upper income counties. According to one source, the 11th graders here abuse prescriptions at twice the national average. Six students in this group, (one in ten) acknowledged visiting someone in prison. One girl said it was her dad, a boy, his uncle, and both were there on drug-related offenses. As they leave, one boy says "thanks," and a girl asks what she should do if she thinks her friend has a drug problem. But it's no surprise, nothing stunning: Drug use has been prevalent among adolescents since I was one, and, if you can imagine back that far, even longer ago than that.

In my first book, *Defining Moments: A Suburban Father's Journey Into his Son's Oxy Addiction*, I told my story: There were hot rods and fist fights and fat bags of marijuana, Hawaii beaches, long hair, hot tubs, and cocaine. Then my brother was addicted, and he went to prison, and there, but for the grace of god and yadda yadda yadda. Something drove me the other way, and I cleaned up pretty well, luckily stumbling down the correct direction on the proverbial "Y" in the road, which was a good thing for me because across that cheesy bar with the phone on every table in 1981, there was Lisa. Then, there was a wedding, a legit career, one son and then another. I was a soccer dad, paying the mortgage on a nice house in a posh suburb. I had come through all sorts of shit and managed to never let it get the best of me. I had it made.

Or had I? My eldest went and got himself addicted to prescription painkillers, and I made every mistake in the book to fix it. I ignored it; I trusted every doctor without question and hoped it would solve itself. I took matters into my own hands and tried to detox him at home. I went undercover, put my own life at risk, and busted a dealer to keep my son out of prison, only to find him high as a kite the very next morning. Our family unit was a disaster and my lofty goals for my eldest son were vanishing before my eyes and being replaced by a simple wish that he would live to see and feel sobriety.

With all I knew, with all I had seen, when my eldest was a teenager, what I thought I knew too much about to allow to happen in my own home happened. In a big way. Drug addiction. Deceit. Repugnant behavior. It could happen in any house. It could happen in yours. Right now. That's why I published *Defining Moments*.

After the release of *Defining Moments*, I went on an unplanned expedition through the lives of many families afflicted by addiction. I was called upon to speak to groups, and I have never turned down a venue, because I quickly came to understand the power of knowledge and awareness and appreciate also the cathartic release of demons. As I had come from a family afflicted by addiction, as the brother of an addict, son of an addict, and now the father of an addict, I came to understand that I could help others know they are not alone and potentially help others avoid the mistakes so many of us who are afflicted by addiction have made. You know hindsight? That omniscient voice that tells you what you should have seen coming before you did? It's hard to silence it now. Sometimes my hindsight voice is so freaking loud that I forget I did it all wrong.

During this period, the epidemic of prescription drug abuse has been sweeping our nation and killing our children at a pace so rapid that deaths by overdose in 2011 exceeded deaths by auto accidents for the first time ever since they began tracking these statistics in the early 1970's. This epidemic continues to grow and as the body count rises, parents look the other way silently mumbling "not my child" while others bury theirs.

The longer my book was out, the more calls I received, and soon the calls were coming from rehab centers, teachers, media, interventionists and other professionals in the business of treating the addicted. A silent demon was lurking. The book and the message appealed to them because I am a father, a man, and someone who was willing to openly admit how addiction defined me, how I thought I knew it all and how I failed. I can admit the many mistakes I made every single day that enabled my child to continue abusing drugs. My kid was falling deeper and deeper into addiction while I thought I was helping him. I've heard it over and over with parents in the calls I've received: We are actually enabling our kids to use, and killing them with kindness, as is completely natural for parents. The easiest thing to do is judge someone else and I don't judge you, I am you!

Parents call me because: My message appeals to them. I can admit I am affected and defined by addiction. I can admit I enabled my child to continue using. But I can see when the parents who call me are doing the same thing, and I call them on it. They might hate to be called on it. I am calling them out. I am calling you out.

I began speaking at high schools and assemblies and classrooms. Sometimes the audience was a freshman class and other times the parents and their children would fill the auditorium. The invitations to speak were beginning to take up a lot of my time, but I knew the impact I was having on these kids and their parents might cause them to travel a different path than the dark journey that might otherwise await them. I also began speaking at professional organizations like Rotary clubs and at support groups.

I bare my soul in radio and TV interviews, public speaking forums, documentaries and individually speaking to family members all over the country hoping to spread awareness about the epidemic of prescription drug abuse. Unfortunately, the individual families I speak to are usually in the throes of addiction and all I can offer them is the knowledge that they are not alone, and the advice to seek professional help immediately. I have learned so much from these families of addicts and addicts themselves. I see the overlapping mistakes. I feel like I could finish their sentence as they describe the behavior of the addict among them. Again and again I see that others have made the same mistakes I made.

Also, I have attempted to build a forum through my website RxDrugAddict.com and communicate through blogs and newsletters. Again, I hope that my efforts will help others to understand that they are not alone but more importantly, I hope that this book opens your eyes and allows you to keep your child from becoming a drug addict through the knowledge I have gained from so many who suffer the consequences of their denial.

When I speak to a crowd, people who have read *Defining Moments* often approach me and tell me that my speech is very different than the book I wrote. In my presentations, I spend more time talking about the causes, symptoms, and awareness of these drugs and addictive behavior than how addiction has defined me as a father, which was really the subject of my first book.

I wasn't setting out to release a book when I first began writing what became *Defining Moments*; it was purely a cathartic release of persistent thoughts. These were the thoughts that woke me in the middle of the night or wouldn't allow me to sleep at all; the thoughts that originally haunted me as I sat in a truck with a wire running up my back, surrounded by undercover narcotic officers I couldn't see. During the drug bust, I had a lot of time to think about every aspect of my life, and contemplate what brought me to that parking lot. Sound was not permitted in my truck because a stereo playing would interfere with the wire intended to capture the incriminating conversation between myself and the drug dealers in that bizarre exchange for my son's freedom for treatment. The silence quite simply made me an easy target for the endless stream of thoughts. All of these memories flowed with the force of a firehose through my mind, and these were my defining moments.

That book was very helpful for me to write, and, based on the feedback I've received from others, valuable to them as well. But it couldn't be all I wrote. I was driven by the need to keep talking and listening and gathering valuable information from others who have lived through the hell of addiction with a child or loved one. I needed to share any new insight with everyone I could in any way possible.

I learned that my book had touched people in a way that helped them open up. They saw the benefit that could come from sharing what had been their dirty little secrets. Both adults and teenagers who I have talked to in groups, assemblies, on the phone and individually in person, tell stories of how their family has been afflicted by addiction, and these stories are so profound and oddly similar that I have felt it necessary to distill these similarities and convey it to others. I am forever grateful for the stories these strangers chose to share, as it is not easy to relive the darkest moments of your life.

I welcome every call from a parent, family member, or addict who contacts me, and I personally reply to every email and make the phone call if they included their number. By this point, I have spoken with literally hundreds of parents and addicts who have shared their story. This book is my letter to those who I cannot reach and those who will not call. Hopefully this book is a letter to those who don't need to call...Yet.

I am not a doctor with a degree in addiction and a two year old. I have grown up as a child surrounded by addiction and drugs, and I was defined by those experiences. I made it through the rabbit hole with my immediate family still intact.

For this book, I personally interviewed an ex-prostitute, a inmate at a maximum security prison, a mother who found the lifeless body of her son in their home, and a family who answered their door to a policeman and a chaplain, knowing precisely why they stood on their front step, and far too many others to list. They were willing to share their dirty little secrets to hopefully help someone else. I urge anyone to disclose their dirty little secret to professionals who can address the disease of addiction. Addictive substances can be found on every corner, in the corner grocery store, in every high school, prescribed to you by your doctor, and sitting innocently in a growing number of households.

I felt compelled to write this book because I have learned so much from speaking to so many parents and family members over the last year. I have been urged by readers who have heard me speak or read my interviews to share my knowledge of the signs, symptoms and perils of drug abuse and addiction.

I write this addition to *Defining Moments* in an attempt to share what I have learned from our plight and the plight of others afflicted by addiction. Occasionally I have presented a composite of several families to avoid redundancies, or created a dramatization, and in all but one case where I have noted it in the text, the true identity of the players has been disguised with the slight alteration of facts to protect them. My hope is that this book can be a resource and perhaps provide some tools to stop addiction at its early stages while some control is still possible. While successful treatment is still probable. While a family is still intact and will grow old together and bounce a grandchild on their knee. Many I have met will never have that opportunity.

I wish I knew then what I know now. Famous last words. I know that many people will not really hear my message, convinced that this is not at all about them, not their child. I can only hope that the families who raise their young children now will never go through the hell so many families have experienced, instead learning from our mistakes and heading addiction off at the early stages or avoiding it all together. My hope is that my book might be a good place to start talking with your children.

I also know that no matter what you read and how hard you try to prevent, detect, and end addiction, that some of you will still end up with an addict among you, just as some will end up with another disease you never anticipated. You can read all you want about cancer, avoid all the risk factors associated with it and you may still find yourself fighting for your life. Education and awareness will reduce your chances of contracting any disease, and that is as good as it gets.

Chapter 1: How I became an advocate for prescription drug awareness

I was doing some self-promotion in conjunction with the release of my book, and had been the subject of a feature story in the local alternative newspaper. In addition to this, after Brandon had come through drug rehab so successfully, I had given them my number as a reference to provide to other potential patient's families. I began to receive letters, emails and phone calls immediately.

Dear Mr. DeHaven,

I started reading your book, Defining Moments *on Tuesday evening and could not put it down. I started reading out loud to my wife Sharon and our high school son TJ that night, then Sharon read the rest to me the next morning & we finished reading together with TJ last night. For being a first time writer you did an unbelievable job. I honestly couldn't wait to finish, I could not put the book down!!*

I will buy several copies and give to the parents we know that have kids becoming teens. After reading this book with my son, TJ told us that he has two friends and knows several other kids that are hooked on Oxy. He told us about one of his friends that is hooked on Oxy and heroin. After reading your book it now makes sense. TJ stayed and listened and I hope that he heard your message loud and clear. We have had many discussions about drugs like crack, oxy, heroin, and that you can't just try those drugs. Your book should have sent an even bigger message that there is far more to addiction than we all think. It's something they will deal with all their lives. This is a growing epidemic and your book will hopefully help many people and help us all watch for signs and stop problems before they start drugs. It took a lot of courage to tell your story and thank you so much for sharing. I hope your son Brandon continues to stay clean and his life gets back to normal. You have all been through so much, many would have crumbled. But you have fought through all your adversities and I admire you for how you have dealt with everything.

As a side note, I really enjoyed reading about your early years; you have overcome so many adversities and done a great job at being a father and husband. I thought I had a tough upbringing, mine pales in comparison. I really liked the story about how you met your wife, Lisa, as that was very touching. Many of the other stories in your past played such an important role in framing the message of the long term devastation drug abuse can have on a family.

God Bless you both,

Mr. H

And another, which emphasized to me how prevalent this problem really was:

Hello Brad, I found you last night online, my name is Jane, I'm in my fifties, raising my grandson alone. I live in south Florida. I do not do drugs, but have gotten an education on them the hard way. I will try and condense this, but I have so very much to say. My daughter got involved (2004/2005) with a family who were the largest suppliers of Oxy, Roxy, and other r/x drugs, in Palm Beach County. These are very dangerous people. She married one of their sons, had a baby boy in July 2006. She came back home to me many times out of fear, but was always threatened to return and she was afraid for her life and that of her baby. They had her doctor shopping and turning all of the drugs over to them. She became addicted over time but she started by doing the drugs so the doctors blood work would show she was taking her prescribed meds so that they would keep prescribing to her. There were 6 adults living in their home and to this date 4 out of 6 have died. In early 2008, my daughter, age 23, died (overdose). Six months after she passed, my husband walked out on me from all the stress in our lives. In December 2008, her husband, age 22, died (overdose). Five months later in 2009 her husband's mother died age 44, (overdose) and later in 2009, my grandson's aunt, age 19, died (overdose). The day my daughter passed, the other family took my grandson and would not let me see him. I tried to save my girl, but I was alone in this fight and they were capable of anything, so I backed off trying to get my grandson. I used all of the money I had trying to get her out and safe, but she died anyway. I got so far behind on everything that I am losing my home of 17 years. As these criminals died off, I knew that I was getting closer to seeing my grandson, maybe getting him back for me to raise and get him away from this Hell, I could feel it. All that was left of their family was the grandfather of my grandchild and his 20 yr. old son, and they were getting tired of dealing with a child. I saw my grandson for the first time again in January 2010 after two years. When I got the call that I could have this sweet boy, he had 60% hearing loss from untreated ear infections; he could not breathe well from untreated nasal infections, and an abscessed broken front tooth. He could not talk, was still in diapers and had been neglected. He was empty of any emotion or love. I have had him almost 2 years now and after many, many doctors' appointments and surgery for his ears and throat, he is in kindergarten now and above average in skills and doing great. My grandson is amazing and he is my hero. I could not save my daughter but I did save her son. I truly congratulate you on saving your son; I feel like I saved the only person I could, my grandson. I know the Love. Kind regards, Jane

I take calls all the time from parents who are in the throes of addiction and I learn so much while I give them an anonymous shoulder to cry on or just someone to talk to who will not judge them in their confusion about addiction and desperation for help. Sometimes I can't help but cry with them, as I truly feel their pain. Some, I'll never forget. You'll find some of them, provided anonymity, through this book.

The first call I received was from a single parent, the mom of a twenty year-old heroin addict. I was at my home and took the call outside. I pace when I talk so I walked all around the backyard. I think I circled the pool about ten times. I talked with her for about an hour. Her son, like mine, started on prescription pain killers that he got from a friend, but several years had passed, and now he had spent all the money he could find, steal, or con and was injecting heroin. She had no idea that a prescription drug could lead to heroin. Many prescription pain killers are, in fact, basically the same drug as heroin. (See Figure 1: Opiates: physiological effects and abuse)

I shared my story with her about my son and they were so parallel. I felt sad for her as she described trying to contact her ex-husband to help pay for rehab and he wanted nothing to do with it, instead telling her that the son just needed to stop using—as if that works. She was puzzled by all the representations from rehab centers. She wanted to get him help, but she didn't have the $30k plus that most places wanted. I tried to calm her the best I could, as I knew she felt completely alone and lost. Heroin was a word she never thought she would utter about her son. I knew she was in a place she never imagined. We've never talked since, so I don't know what happened to her. I do know that she never saw addiction coming, and that is the primary thing we all have in common.

Sometimes, parents send me pictures of their children before they were drug addicts. These are some of the most difficult conversations I have. The parents are grieving, wondering what happened, many times uncertain whether they will ever see their children alive again. Sometimes their addicted children have disappeared into the underbelly, out somewhere on the streets, leaving the parents waiting for that phone call or that knock at the door that will give them any information. The pictures they hang on to are of their children posed with a baseball bat high in the air, wearing a hat that looks three sizes too big, smiling from ear to ear, grinning through "cheese." The pictures are of their child healthy and happy laughing with friends and family as a young teen or newly morphed adult. Unfortunately, it is also the case that pictures like these appear in the obituaries, after an overdose or suicide; and these parents have connected with me also. The agony doesn't disappear once a child is no longer living. The need to share is just as strong; their desire to help others is usually stronger.

Opiates: physiological effects and abuse

Oxycontin	Heroin
synthetic; derived from opium poppy	synthetic; derived from opium poppy
receptors in the body to reduce the perception of pain	receptors in the body to reduce the perception of pain
produces drowsiness, mental confusion, nausea, and can depress respiration	produces drowsiness, mental confusion, nausea, and can depress respiration
creates euphoric response	creates euphoric response
swallowed, snorted, melted/liquefied, injected, smoked	swallowed, snorted, melted/liquefied, injected, smoked

Figure 1

Thankfully, people don't just share their tragedies with me. Our family has come so far and been so fortunate. Although we had weathered a horrific relapse in August 2010 and Brandon was sent back to rehab, he completed the program in December 2010 (More on this, in Chapter 12), by July 4, 2011, my two sons were home; we were all living under one roof again, and a sense of cautious optimism had resumed, a feeling of normalcy, that all was well with the world. So, we hosted a Fourth of July party at our home. Our boys, now twenty-four and twenty-six, invited many friends who were swimming, laughing and just having a great time. I didn't know the names of many of the young adults in attendance but I took great joy as a fly on the wall as I just floated around the pool and watched the interaction and dynamic of all of these "kids."

As I floated towards the steps in the pool, a young man swam up to me. He had longer hair (like I did in the 70's) and he just floated up next to me as I watched the young people play laugh and chat. He said, "You don't know me but I read your book."

I said, "So where did you get it from?"

He replied, "My college roommate, who got it from your younger son."

I said, "So what did you think?"

He went on to tell me that he, now twenty-four years old, was once a drug addict—an Oxy addict. He finally decided to go into rehab when he realized that his life sucked, and he didn't want to live the life of an addict anymore. So he embraced rehab, and focused on removing drugs from his life, and getting his life together. It wasn't easy for him, he told me, as he was in a band on tour. Drugs were always present and offered to him almost daily when he was on the road. But he made a commitment to himself and he now loved his life clean and sober.

He said, "I was hurt that my father didn't call me after rehab and congratulate me for finally being clean, so I never called him. I hadn't talked to my father or the rest of my family in a couple of years since as our relationship was essentially over." I listened, and he continued, "When I read your book, I realized what a selfish little ass I had been. How much I had hurt my family and how needy I was always calling my dad to bail me out and send me money every time I got in trouble. After I read your book it hit me as to all the bad I had done and that it was not up to my dad to reach out to me with congratulations for being sober, but it was up to me to call him and make amends with my family for how badly I had hurt them and for all the stress I must have caused them." He finished with the best thing he could have possibly said to me: "I called my father within an hour of finishing your book and we are talking again and I know I have a lot to do to try to make things right between me and my family, but we are communicating and that is a great start. Thanks for writing the book and for being brutally honest about how life can even be tough for fathers."

Now, I have had a lot of conversations with people of all ages, but this one really hit me. I realized that my story moved this young man to realize something about himself, to take ownership of his actions, realize how his addiction wasn't just affecting himself and to reunite him with his family. I don't think it gets much better than that!

I simply said to him, "I would have written and published this book just to hear your comment. Thank you."

I've started to think of this public speaking and book writing, my prescription drug abuse awareness advocacy, as a calling. It started as a desire to let those afflicted by addiction know that they are not alone; there is professional help. I hope I can put my arms around these tattered families and offer some form of relief, but at the end of the day when the lights turn out they wonder where it all went wrong and they grieve for what they cannot change and they bear the weight of wishing they knew then what they know now.

The number one question I am asked during all of the speaking engagements and interviews is: "How is your son?" Perfect strangers ask me this question. I truly appreciate that question, and believe that it illustrates how much people care. Being a first time writer, I truly had no clue as to the many ways my story would touch so many people from so many walks of life. From young to old, addicted to afflicted and everything in between, the conversations, reviews, email and personal talks I have had with these readers has touched me deeply, as I discover how my story affected them on so many levels.

I have also learned that it is far more difficult for me to personally stand in front of an audience and bare my soul than it was to write it down. When I am writing, I sit alone in front of my computer, and as I read my words or stumble upon something about myself, I can shed a tear quietly without notice. When I stand on a stage and the emotions surface as I tell the audience about my darkest moments in an attempt to spare them the hell I went through or to help them through the hell they are living, I fight back the tears—sometimes unsuccessfully. I thought at first that it would get easier over time and that it wouldn't tear me up to share those memories, but I was wrong. Each time I show the withdrawals video, I suffer real physical pain, and have to turn away.

The obvious question is, why do I continue to torment myself with these events? The answer is easy: I feel as though my street-level insight into addiction may help those who are in the throes of addiction, so they know that they are not alone and will hopefully seek the professional help they need. Better yet, maybe I am able to raise the awareness of those with young, as of yet unaffected, children, and provide them with the tools they need to notice the signs of drug abuse early, take the steps necessary to curtail access to prescription medications and hopefully keep them from ever experiencing addiction. I hope the younger children who listen to me will realize that they are not invincible and they are one snort, one puff, one experiment away from discovering whether they will become addicted. Nobody ever tries a drug with the intention of becoming an addict and destroying their life. I had no idea that I would ever write a book when I began pecking away at my laptop. Once I released the book, all my deepest darkest dirty little secrets were essentially carved in stone for all to read. And when I thought I was finished, my work had just begun.

Chapter 2: What is stigma? Exposing the dirty little secret

When we became aware of our son Brandon's problem, my wife Lisa and I closed the doors, drew the drapes, and tried to handle it ourselves. At the worst moments, we completely shut out our family and friends, alone, ashamed and helpless. We cancelled family holidays with lame excuses so as not to let my in-laws become aware of Brandon's addiction. It wasn't until I reached out to my mother, and in a more complicated fashion, my brother, not until we went out and put ourselves out there for help that we got it.

One of the most important things I feel I can do is to help eradicate the stigma and promote the idea that this is a disease and not a dirty little secret. This is a message my wife, my son and I would have benefited from back when the issue reared its head in our home.

"Sheri and David"

Not too long ago, I received a call from a woman I'll call "Sheri." As hard as Sheri tried, her words were garbled by tears. She called me after finding my website, and she needed answers to questions she couldn't even articulate.

"Calm down Sheri," I interjected. "I'll do the talking, OK?"

I have learned through all the calls that I have had, that I can calm the caller down and get them more in control with a few simple questions, preferably requiring a very brief one word answer: Is the addict in your life a son or a daughter? What is his/her name? How old is he/she (now using the name of the child)? What is the drug of choice? How long has he/she been addicted? Did this addiction start due to an injury with prescription drugs prescribed by a doctor or was it recreational? Now we are talking.

She tells me about her son, who we'll call "David," a twenty year old who has been addicted to Oxy and heroin for two years, since receiving a prescription for an injury. "He just couldn't stop and found stronger and stronger drugs," she said.

Sheri is a single mom, whose best friend is her sister, but they hadn't talked much lately because Sheri couldn't bear the thought of telling her sister that David is a heroin addict. Sheri told me the shame she felt over her son's addiction, and she felt like a failure. These are two things I understand all too well. I asked her to tell me more about her sister. Sheri said that they were very close, and even their sons had been born about a year apart. I am not a trained psychologist, but I have spoken to hundreds of parents who are in the deepest darkest moments of their life and they pour their heart out to me and they need what my wife and I needed, simply someone to talk to who wouldn't be judgmental, someone who has been in their shoes.

I told Sheri, "Your sister has a son the same age as your son, so she will know this problem is out there. She may even know other families with addicts, friends of your nephew. I talk to a lot of people and I can tell that you need your best friend. Call her and reach out to her for your sanity because your son's addiction is destroying you and you need your sister." Sheri agreed and we ended our call.

A few hours later, Sheri called back. She was bawling, but in a way I can describe as relieved. Sheri had just hung up from a long call with her sister, where she had discovered the unbelievable. Sheri's nephew, her sister's son, had been in rehab for two months for heroin addiction, and her sister had been too ashamed to call her best friend and sister, Sheri. At a time when these two sisters—mothers and best friends—needed each other more than ever before, the stigma of addiction and the need to keep the dirty little secret had robbed them of the much needed support they could have had in each other.

I felt so happy to have been a part of this reunion, hopefully facilitating some kind of healing.

The moral of the story is this: You are not alone. This is an epidemic. Your best friend might be dealing with this, but you'll never know unless you reach out. We need to talk to other loved ones about our experiences and stop the madness of the dirty-little-secret mentality. A stigma is, after all, an ever-changing target.

Early in *Defining Moments* I talked about the stigma of teenage pregnancy for my own mother in the late 1950's. I did this for a reason. Stigma will always be and has always been present. A wide variety of illnesses and human conditions were sources of shame before they were accepted as ways of being, conditions, or illness worthy of research and requiring treatment and/or compassion. A child with Down Syndrome was institutionalized, deaf people considered dumb, epilepsy or an epileptic family member a source of shame, people with birth defects shunned. More recently, people who couldn't control their drinking were seen as weak, bad drunks, cigarette smokers as having no willpower, homosexuality as a perversion to be hidden. Then there's the stigma of having cancer, or AIDS, or an eating disorder. And all the stigmas surrounding pregnancy: A visibly pregnant teenager "walking down the aisle;" the same teenager raising the child on her own as a single mom; baby's daddy and mommy-to-be deciding to not get married and "live in sin." And now, there is the stigma of addiction, as if an addict set out to be the best addict they could be. Addicts are sick, and need professional help, and although many of the formerly stigmatized conditions I mentioned are now accepted as within the range of normal, in some cases, where it is warranted, treatment even covered by insurance, addiction for the most part is not.

Sure, this insurance company or that may give you a thirty-day treatment (could you imagine a doctor who said, "You've got cancer and your policy covers thirty days of treatment? A thirty day addiction "treatment" is throwing a Band-Aid at a severed artery!); families without resources have little choice when the very prescription medicines their insurance companies helped them buy have their children stealing family jewelry and selling their body on the street to satisfy the demon of addiction. It is absolutely absurd that addiction is not treated like the disease it is. I and many others will continue to beat this drum until the stigma of addiction is a distant memory. We as a society will deny it until we accept it as we always have, and we always will.

Talk to erase the stigma. Talk, and ye shall connect.

"Debbie T. and Brandon"

I took a wrong turn in this small town. Redding, California wasn't yielding me any friendly faces, and the frontage road I was driving on was mostly deserted. I noticed a local hotel with a no-name diner attached to it. The parking lot was full of trucks, and that is a good sign in any small town.

I made my way in through the front door, collected a few stares from the locals and headed towards a large curved bar. If I'm eating alone and a place has a bar, there is no better place to sit and eat. You aren't the one person taking up a whole table, and you are almost guaranteed quick service and a little conversation as the bartender can't escape.

My bartender was a lady, her name was a nickname, and a collection of her first and last name combined. She was sweet and attentive. I had to pass on her meal recommendation, which I rarely do, but since it was smothered in onions and my next financial planning appointment was with a dental office, I felt they had likely endured enough bad breath so I would spare them mine. The bartender was eating something behind the bar in-between filling the drink orders from the table servers. As far as I remember, I was the only patron at the bar. I couldn't resist a little icebreaker because I tend to be a bit of a chatty-Cathy so I asked her what she was eating, to which she answered "pot stickers in hot wing sauce." Well this chatty-Cathy is also a bit of a jokester/smartass so I said, "So, that must mean you are pregnant!"

She laughed and said, "Hardly, I've had all the kids I'll ever have, my youngest is 18."

When I asked her how many children she has, she answered, "I had three."

Well, I knew there was a story there since she used the word "had" but I skipped by it because there can be nothing good in that story. I am a stranger and I know she owes me no further explanation. She said, "How many do you have?" And I answered that I have two sons, one twenty-four and one twenty-six and a wife of twenty-seven years. She replied, "I've been married twenty seven years also; got married in May, 1984." It turned out we had the same marriage date and the same number of years. She said, "My 'had' would have been twenty-six, his name was Brandon."

I replied, of course, that my twenty-six year old was named Brandon also.

She gathered up close across from me on the opposite side of the bar, her eyes welled a bit and she said, "Brandon died of a drug overdose last year. Ten days after his birthday, his girlfriend Tiffany found him dead, and it was a week after I kicked him out for stealing my medication."

I said, "I wrote a book about my son Brandon. He was an Oxy addict and his girlfriend's name was also Tiffany."

I'm sure the coincidence gave us both goose bumps. Our lives seemed to be lining up parallel, with one very important exception—my son was alive. She began to open up to me about the pain of her loss and the guilt that she carried for kicking him out, only to lose him a week later. She asked me how she could get my book, and if I thought it might help her and her husband. I told her I had a book in the car and it would be my pleasure to give it to her, but that I had no idea if it would help her or not. She said softly, "My Brandon was tall with the brightest blue eyes...yours?"

"The same," I said. "Tall. With eyes that light up a room they are so blue."

She put her hands across the counter touching mine and said, "I would love to read your book."

After I ate, I retrieved a book for her, signed it, and wished her the best of luck. Had I really taken a wrong turn in Redding? No way. She and I have talked, texted and met personally on another occasion, and she asked me to share this story with you. Her name is Debbie T, but you can call her Debit.

Chapter 3: Why it helps to acknowledge that addiction is a disease

Addicts are sick. Why did I snort coke alongside my brother yet he became an addict like our father and I didn't? To scientifically argue that addiction is a disease is beyond the scope of this book, but anecdotal evidence in my experience leads me to believe that there is a genetic inclination towards addiction just as there is a genetic inclination towards diabetes, cancer, heart disease, etc. And once one has contracted the disease, it can no more be treated at home with home remedies than can a huge tumor on your neck.

When he was fifteen, my child broke his arm on a trampoline and was prescribed Vicodin. Three years later, he was a junkie. Perhaps the doctor should have asked about my family history, or maybe I should have said loud and clear: "My brother is an Opiate addict and my father an alcoholic!" But I simply didn't know that this was relevant, because I believed that my brother and father couldn't control themselves and were addicts by their own doing. They had some character flaw, some hole in their emotional lives, some gap their parents left unfilled, and it was because of this that they became addicts. They kept using because they were weak. My theory, however, fell apart with my son, who had me not only for a devoted dad, but also for a soccer coach, etc. and he wanted for nothing. I was so wrong to believe it couldn't be my kid.

Honor students, class presidents, leaders of the debate team, cheerleaders and sports stars are not exempt from addiction. Oh, you're wealthy and live in a nice neighborhood? Your kids go to the best schools? So you are exempt from having a child who becomes a heroin addict instead of a CEO? Nope. These children are just as likely, perhaps more likely, to get a prescription for an injury or drink a little too much at a party when some friend says, "Hey, try this pill, it will make you feel better," or, "We don't need beer because Sally got these pills from her Grandpa's house, and they will make you feel drunk;" the list of possible scenarios is endless, and it would be absurd to try to imagine them all here.

In the end, an addict will go from their million dollar home in suburbia or their average apartment in the 'hood and crawl into the deep dark pockets of our cities and they will find their opiate, they will find their heroin, because their body will not allow them to deny it.

My son went from a community with a median income higher than Beverly Hills to the slums of Tijuana to score heroin because his body could not survive without it.

Addiction all starts with a flip of the coin. If I try "drug X" will my body enjoy the feeling? Will I continue to desire this feeling, and will there come a time when my body says if you don't give me "drug X" I will punish you? The experimenters are the ones in power—until they are powerless, and it can happen in an instant. Addiction must be addressed early because it doesn't just go away. It is the tumor of addiction growing on the side of their neck and it needs treatment, or it will only grow worse until they are lying on the floor, convulsing in withdrawals when they go too long between fixes.

An addict will live with this addiction even after remission. It will hibernate. It will rear its head at inopportune and unexpected moments: Five years from now the prescription drug addict in remission must have a tooth pulled without medication because introducing that pain killer back into his body could awaken the demon of addiction that sleeps inside.

I used to have a side-business that sold calling cards to small markets and liquor stores. The worse the neighborhood the better the sales, because a lot of these people who came to these establishments had no phone, so a calling card was a necessity. Most patrons had no cars—these were neighborhood dive stores. As I would wait to speak to the owner, I would watch the customers, and to my amazement they would buy these small bottles of alcohol that were pocket size for about half the cost of a bottle four times the size or more. Sometimes they would sign their names or ask the owner if they could put the purchase on their credit account until they received their once-monthly check. The business owner would pull out a binder, locate their name—which he knew by memory—and jot down the debt. I asked about this arrangement at several stores as this transaction confused me for several reasons: Why would the business owner give credit to what seemed to me to be a high-risk client, and why would the patron spend so much on so little when they could go to a discount or grocery store and get multiples of that quantity for a bit more? The owners all told me basically the same thing: first off, the customer didn't have the money to go to a discount store and, more importantly, if they did, and they purchased a half gallon of booze, they might be dead tomorrow because they would drink everything they had on them.

The small bottle was a way for these alcoholics to pace themselves, economics be damned. They had come to understand that once they open a bottle of booze they were not done until the bottle was empty, so a smaller bottle meant they would be back the next day for the same. As far as an extension of credit, the owners said they rarely had issues with non-payment because eventually the customers would get their money and they would want to show they would pay because a day would come when they needed their nightly bottle and they would have no money—keeping their tab paid up was a method of future survival. They also were not judged here; the owner knew the deal, and the little bottles were profitable so even if some deadbeats didn't pay, he would make money in the end. I'm sure these people never planned on this being their nightly ritual, but it was, and they maintained for another night, to live another day. An addict lives for today and hopes to make it to tomorrow. All other goals are second and last.

"Stacy" (WARNING: SEXUALLY EXPLICIT)

One of the most disturbing interviews I did was with a young woman I'll call "Stacy." She told me about the day she started doing the unimaginable for drugs: On that day, back when she was sixteen years old, Stacy entered the small, dark motel room and saw small mattresses and bedding all over the room. A towel was tossed on the dirty carpet between two twin mattresses on the floor. The large man who let her in handed her $30 and she gripped it. Her cell phone was on, and she knew her boyfriend/pimp Leroy could hear everything. The man reached for his belt and motioned Stacy to the towel on the ground, telling her to lay on her back the best he could in his broken English but she understood. He pulled up her dress almost covering her face as he dropped to his knees in front of her and pried her legs apart with his callused hands. He crawled on top of her and she cried, and he took sick pleasure in it, as he looked her straight in the eyes and pumped away at her body. She tried to look away only to see the doors of the other rooms open as what seemed like a dozen men watched, some standing just behind the one that was inside of her now. The men behind him cheered and jeered as he fucked her and she could see the wads of cash in the hands of the men in line behind him, they all seemed to be readying themselves for the same as pants were dropped and arms were moving. In a matter of seconds, the man on top of her finished. He said something derogatory in Spanish and motioned the next in line towards her naked body. As the first man crawled off, the next man moved in, ordered her to her knees, handed her $30, and mounted her from behind. By the time she left the room she had $210 in her hand and had been raped by seven different men. When she entered this room she had only had sex with one man, Leroy, and this was her first time prostituting herself, but it would be far from the last.

The drugs she was addicted to had her head spinning, and the situation had her young mind confused. She walked to Leroy's car and his first words were, "Give me the money, all of it!" She begged to go home, to no avail. She was now his whore and he her pimp. Stacy knew without exception that when she stepped into Leroy's car they were headed to the apartment complexes that dotted a poor area of town where customers, "Johns" were plentiful, and many times there were more than a dozen to a room. There were nights she handed Leroy up to $6000; she never saw one penny but he kept her high, usually shoving another pill in her mouth as she returned to his car with another wad of cash. She took up to eight pills a night. In the mornings she would find the bruises on her body and she was in such pain that she could hardly walk.

Believe it or not, she went to high school, and lied to her mom to go out at night. Her body craved the drugs that would help her through another night of prostitution and drugs that would help her not feel the pain and reality of what she had become. The pills were dispensed like a pellet to a rat from the window of Leroy's car, but only after all the money was handed to him. She was lying, cheating, addicted and selling her body on the street in dark rooms with a line of scumbags gang banging her for money.

She told me, "I was a rich white girl from Roseville one day and a drug addicted hooker a week later."

Addicts don't do the shit they do because it's fun. They don't do it for attention. They do it because of a physical compulsion, a physical withdrawal that is so excruciatingly painful it outweighs any other need. This, by my definition, is certainly an illness.

The stigma of addiction perpetuates a belief that an addict sets out with a goal of becoming an addict. It's not like they are sitting around one day and say, "Hey, I think I'll snort this line and if I get really good at this, I could be addicted or dead in a few years."

This is a disease, and I don't believe they have found a cure for it yet. Uninformed people consider this a self-inflicted wound and therefore they have a difficult time accepting this diagnosis. With most people they make a very simple suggestion/question: "Why don't they just stop?" I and millions of others, including the addicts themselves, wish it was that simple.

It used to be that people thought that someone who was a "bad drunk" just couldn't keep up with their fellow drinkers and were of weak character. Alcoholism has, within the last decade or so, begun to be recognized as a disease to which some are genetically predisposed. Cirrhosis and liver cancer are now understood to be potential by-products of alcohol abuse. Alcohol used to sit on the credenzas of the offices across the country, right next to the fancy cocktail glasses, adjacent to the ashtrays and fancy cigarette lighters. Speaking of cigarettes, these too were once believed to be non-addictive and harmless, but now we accept that addiction and lung cancer may be a result of use. There is no question that lung cancer is a disease. Our healthcare system pays for every penny of cancer treatment, as it should. It also often pays for smoking cessation programs. Now, laws have changed; information is up; smoking is down—for 12th graders, from forty percent in 1997 to twenty percent in 2009! Skin cancer for the sun worshiper, diabetes for the overeater. I could go on, but I believe the point is well made because no well person would intentionally destroy themselves in all of these scenarios. Addiction is a disease!

Defining addiction as an illness or a disease is helpful. It was helpful to me, as it allowed me to forgive Brandon. I can look at his behavior and separate it from the person. It has assisted my work-in-progress of forgiving my brother. I am sure my brother Thomas doesn't remember being so high that he wouldn't take his wife to the hospital when she was having a miscarriage. Thomas was strung out, and a hospital was the last place this paranoid drug addict was willing to go. My wife took her, and I stayed with him and their other children.

Believing addiction is an illness, whether or not it can clinically and scientifically be proven to be so, assists the healing process of those affected. Until he receives proper treatment, until he accepts the treatment, uses the tools for health, I cannot help him. Just as I cannot help my friend with his cancer—I can't bear the weight of this.

Treating addiction as an illness will also help address our overcrowded prison system. Too many people in prison are there because of their addiction and money is spent on incarceration instead of treatment to get them out of the cycle. I believe the prison system could reasonably break out a portion of the addicted population and treat their disease, inpatient and guarded, but at a much lower cost than putting these addicts in with the murderers and rapists of

The point is, just acknowledging that these crimes are committed during the act of getting drugs for the addict, and treating the cause of this crime rather than the symptoms, would go a long way.

this world. The protocol for handling an addict would be much less expensive than treating them all under one category as criminals: Just as it is more costly to guard an inmate on death row over the general population, it is more costly to treat addiction-crime related inmates in with the general population. I believe in creating a system whereby those who committed a crime to feed their addiction are put into a drug rehabilitation program that stops the cycle of abuse. It is madness to treat them like animals for fifteen years, then release them and expect them to stay clean. Drugs are easily accessible in prison, so in a lot of cases the addicted inmate in the general population never stops using; so, how do we expect them to act in our society when they are eventually free? It could be a privilege to be in the program: Ramifications for disruptive prisoners in a rehabilitation prison could include shipping their ass back to real prison if they don't comply. Conditions of parole could be specific for drug abusers. This is not pie in the sky thinking here. We might save money at the state and federal level, treat people with a disease so they can walk our streets and work beside us productively and contribute instead of drain our communities and hold a gun to our head to feed an addiction they never addressed in prison.

As I am writing this book, a fairly high-profile battle over this issue is taking place in the court system. Cameron Douglas, son of actor Michael Douglas, is serving an extended sentence for drug distribution and heroin possession. He is thirty-three years old and began injecting heroin daily in his mid-twenties. He has not received treatment in prison, and according to a New York Times Article on May 21, 2012, "is a textbook example of someone suffering from untreated opioid dependence [for whom] more prison time would do nothing to solve his underlying problems."

Treating any illness or disease with punishment is not the answer. Sure, there are plenty of examples where drug dealers should be in prison. Especially when violence is involved. Still, if someone turns to violence or drug dealing or prostitution to feed an addiction there should be medical treatment as part of their reform.

The State of California spent a lot of time and money to change their name from "The California Department of Corrections" to add "and Rehabilitation" to the end. Did they do more than just change the name? What changed behind the walls? According to the CDCR website, on June 1, 2012, "Twenty-seven inmates from California State Prison-Solano today received certifications that will eventually enable them to counsel other inmates in addiction treatment programs for alcohol and drug abuse." This is something. A start.

The State Prison Corcoran is supposed to work with substance abuse treatment, but it would appear that the availability of this is spotty and the success of these programs is uncertain. Opportunities for rehabilitation are primarily voluntary programs the prisoners can choose to join. They are called Leisure Time and Self Help Activities. A 2010 report on substance use in the prison population, called "Behind Bars II: Substance Abuse and America's Prison Population," found that:

> 84.8 percent of inmates in America are substance involved...Screening can be used to identify those in need of intervention and to make appropriate referrals to treatment, which ultimately can help to reduce crime and prison overcrowding and save taxpayer money...Despite abundant evidence of the efficacy of screening and brief interventions, standardized screening and interventions are not implemented regularly in justice settings...Although inmates are guaranteed the right to medical care, they routinely are denied access to appropriate screening, intervention and treatment services for the disease of addiction.

From what I hear, getting drugs in prison is easier than getting a steak. The *Times* article about Douglas explained that Douglas got his incarceration duration extended because people inside the prison supplied him drugs and he was caught with them. Heroin. Suboxone.

Addicts have an illness. When someone is deeply addicted, they have lost control of the ability to "just say no" and all you need to do is watch the withdrawal video of my son at RxDrugAddict.com to understand that the drug addiction is controlling the body.

No addict ever said, "Hey, I'll smoke that joint; snort that line; or take that pill and if I'm really good at it I'll be addicted and robbing a liquor store within the year." These people have a medical condition that is being ignored, and this is what has motivated a group of physicians to file a brief on behalf of Douglas. We hear about the plight of Cameron Douglas because of his high profile, but the prisons are filled with John and Jane Does who we will never hear about, and so are the morgues. Prison systems could cut costs dramatically and reduce the rate of return offenders if they took the word "rehabilitation" seriously and segregated addicts into treatment centers that were secure without the need to put them in the general population of killers and child sex abusers.

Rehabilitate or Incarcerate? Perhaps a combination of both for addicts who have broken the law is the answer because either we treat the wound or we pour salt in it.

Chapter 4: The Addict Among Us—The unbelievable ways addicts manipulate those who love and trust them

Fortunately or unfortunately, Brandon's drug addiction reconnected me with my brother in an uncomfortable way. The two of them have something in common: They are both addicts, and as we know, they have plenty of company. The difference is that one of them is still young and there is hope for his full recovery, the other, well, not so much in my opinion. When Brandon finally agreed to get treatment the first time, he contacted my brother Thomas who had told us he had connections with Narconon. I'll be honest, it was difficult for me to accept Thomas' help, and Thomas didn't make it any easier by rubbing my face in it every chance he could. I had hoped that Thomas would get his satisfaction from helping his nephew get in to rehab, but I had a lifetime of expecting one thing from my brother and receiving quite the opposite. On the note of saving Brandon, a lot goes into that equation: Brandon was the number one person who saved himself because he had to embrace treatment and then go on to live a life clean from drugs while surrounded by drugs. I contribute a lot of factors to Brandon's recovery, and there are probably some I don't know about: The cops who followed him for two years and eventually busted him; having a gun held to his head and being robbed for his drugs several times; withdrawals when he couldn't afford or find the drugs his body demanded; then there's that crazy dad who went undercover to get him out of a jail stint and keep his option for rehab available; the many wonderful counselors at Narconon; the Narcotics Anonymous (NA) and Alcoholics Anonymous (AA) meetings he attended and the people he met there; the sober living home, good or bad it made him consider his life and his future. No single event or person can be credited with my son being an addict in remission, and that is a simple fact.

After Brandon finished his first stint at rehab, he went to work for my brother down in Southern California doing handy man and construction kinds of jobs. In August 2010, Brandon was celebrating a milestone of sorts: He had been free from Oxy and other opiate drugs for eighteen months. It was also a milestone for my beautiful wife of twenty-six years as her fiftieth birthday approached. I decided to take Lisa on a leisurely road trip down California's coastline on Highway 1 to celebrate the event. We planned to see Brandon in the San Diego area, to enjoy a wonderful dinner with him and celebrate his milestone of being drug free for a year and a half while giving him the opportunity to see his mother and celebrate her birthday.

Back when this all began, the thought of celebrating sobriety with our eldest son seemed like a dream that would never come true, but soon we were with our son who had evolved into a healthy, happy and energetic young man.

I have met too many people who mark the birthday of their drug addicted child wondering what street they are sleeping on, or where they are prostituting themselves. Or perhaps these parents know exactly where their children are, because they are sitting in a prison cell, or worse yet they bring flowers to their child's gravesite and kneel beside the tombstone. Those parents live without their child and every holiday, Mother's Day, Father's Day, or every time they see one of their old friends, or gaze upon a picture on the mantel, they crumble inside. They will never see their children alive again and all of the dreams for that child vanish with their last breath. I count myself among the blessed, for now, because I do have my son back and I did watch it get extremely out of control. My family and I are the lucky ones because we do not mark a family occasion by laying flowers at our child's gravesite thankful only because they are at last in peace.

Brandon's sobriety was the best birthday gift his mother could possibly receive. We enjoyed a wonderful dinner together in downtown San Diego, overlooking the bay. Brandon was a changed person in so many ways. His demeanor was calm and focused, and he was proud of his ability to get clean and stay clean. He was fit and bright eyed with an outlook on life that was positive despite any hurdles that would come his way. Many obstacles had followed him from his past. Those doors of opportunity that had slammed shut in the wake of his behavior as an addict were now revealing how tightly they were sealed and how difficult they would be to pry open, if it could be done at all. He was also facing major dental work due to his years of drug abuse and neglect, but he looked forward to getting these items done, as they say, one day at a time.

Gone was the anorexic frame, the pale and broken-out face, and the baggy dark circles that had once surrounded his now bright blue eyes. It was great to see him like this, as he was living with three clean roommates who were great guys with respectable jobs. Brandon was having a tough time finding a job in the disaster of an economy, and a three-year gap is his résumé wasn't going to help him get a call back despite his willingness to do anything it took.

So Brandon was staying busy doing part time work for both my brother Thomas and my half-brother, Harry. For Harry, Brandon was doing everything from helping him build a gazebo at his home in L.A. to assisting him on photo and video shoots when he was needed. Brandon was helping Thomas with an abundance of landscaping and ditch digging because, as we all know, the world needs ditch diggers. They both paid him well and they were generous with extras, like feeding him and giving him old furniture to help Brandon settle in. Brandon was thrilled to get anything, and continued to look for a real job. His positive outlook in a bleak situation was just one of the signs of his sobriety. (See Figure 2: Signs of a Successful Rehabilitation)

One thing that had become evident as I rejoiced in my son's recovery was that his uncle Thomas was still struggling with issues relating to his various addictions. Despite claiming the contrary, he had never completed the Narconon program. Thomas had inflated his importance and continued to inflate his role in Brandon's treatment process. The issues we had with one another were clearly not resolved, and, to this day, are unresolved. Over the years, he had manipulated me, and I had allowed myself to be manipulated by him. I can complain about the time he sold me a car that he didn't own, but unfortunately, I'd be exposing myself as a fool for buying a car from someone who didn't own it. The addiction, the behavior, is a symptom of deeper-seated problems that only the sufferer can address and eradicate. They lie to others, but most of all they lie to themselves and begin to believe their stories. (See Figure 3: Signs of long term, unsuccessfully treated addiction) Thomas constantly let me down, and I repeatedly allowed him to do so.

There were times we did not talk for several years. These times usually occurred after Thomas relapsed, emotionally hurt my mother, used my home as a drug den, or was abusive in some manner, as he would get violently angry when confronted about his drug abuse. All of these scenarios were usually caused by whatever his new drug of choice was. My brother's addiction seemed to be constantly changing over the decades: Cocaine, pot, opiates like Vicodin and Norco, liquid Hydrocodone, Heroin, gambling—

whatever he could get his hands on to satisfy his addictive personality.

Success: Signs of a Successful Rehabilitation

Signs of a Successful Rehabilitation

Making amends

Calm resignation

Accepting personal responsibility

Respectful behavior

Timeliness and responsibility

A desire to be with family

Working hard and helping others

Figure 2

It was difficult to go out to dinner at a local restaurant and not be approached by someone griping that my brother had burned them in some financial deal. Our phone would ring with strangers asking if we were related to Thomas and if we knew where he was or how to get a hold of him. It just gets old, and I again came to the conclusion that nothing good happens when I am around Thomas just like with my biological father. Thomas was living it up in a big house, eating fancy dinners at expensive restaurants and buying racehorses one month, and facing eviction, broke and hiding from debt collectors the next.

Thomas seemed to me to be living the life of a conman, almost a duplicate of our biological father, Richard. I always found their similarities odd since they truly had little exposure to each other, but they were so much alike that sometimes they would make the exact same bizarre statement. I remember each of them saying to me during confrontation several years apart, "If you don't do X, you'll never see my children again." I remember both times thinking, what about my children? It was all about them, and they played a relationship with their children like a trump card; the fact that I had children who they wouldn't see didn't play into the equation. They didn't care. Addicts really only think about themselves and nothing else matters. If you let your guard down, an addict will take what they can get, plain and simple.

In any case, Thomas was back in my life after Brandon went to him for help. We totally appreciated his assistance getting Brandon into rehab the first time, and I have told Thomas so on many occasions. Unfortunately, Thomas was continually changing the story of how he "paid" to "save Brandon's life." It became very uncomfortable for me to keep hearing. Eventually, I confronted him about this, because Thomas originally told me that Narconon agreed to waive Brandon's $30k fee because of all of the work Thomas had done for Narconon, and all the money that Thomas had donated to them over the years. But his story changed, and a few months later, Thomas told me that he had "spent his last $30k to pay for Brandon's rehab," and then a few months later, Thomas told me this dramatic story about how he had to "liquidate his children's college savings accounts to save Brandon's life."

So I confronted him because I felt like he was lying to me and I didn't understand why. I clarified through Narconon that in fact Brandon's first treatment was pro-bono due to Thomas's relationship with the director of one of the centers.

Again, we are beyond appreciative that Thomas was able to pull those strings and get Brandon the treatment he needed and we are forever grateful, but as I told Thomas, there was no need to lie to me about his financial outlay.

Failure: signs of long term addiction

Signs of long term, unsuccessfully treated addiction

Drama

Disappearing

Mania

Lying

Violent outbursts

Forgetfulness

"Borrowing" money

Ostentatious spending

Figure 3

The way my brother reacted to life, compared to my now rehabilitated son, despite supposedly receiving the same treatment and life strategies, was inexplicably different. Thomas' inclination to lying and deception, exaggeration and anger, and all the drama I have come to associate with addiction, was concerning and very curious to me. I began investigating the vast difference in my brother Thomas's result in rehab versus my son's and that of so many others I had met. It was then that a head of the Narconon staff told me that my brother never completed their rehabilitation program. I was shocked because of the way Thomas had helped get Brandon into Narconon, and then again, I guess I wasn't that shocked because Thomas was the same asshole he had always been and didn't seem to have the same values and tools that Brandon gained in the program. I realized too that Thomas never made any calls to family members to apologize for the things he had done to us, as is customary with the final stages of treatment at Narconon and many other rehab centers.

As I heard it from the staff, Thomas went through the withdrawals and was transferred to the center for his addiction but very quickly "blew-out" (the term for leaving before completion) because he had too many business deals to complete. This explained a lot of Thomas's behavior, as he truly conned his way out of the program— they cannot keep you as an adult if you want to leave. Thomas had blown out and was still dealing with the demons of addiction without the tools rehab could have given him.

> **Drug addicts will tell you anything they can to get what they need, and this type of action is all part of the sickness of addiction. Lying is a big part of an addict's survival.**

I remember another time when Thomas blew out of a rehab while he still lived in the Sacramento area about ten years ago. I was surprised to get a call from Thomas insisting on meeting me as soon as possible at a nearby restaurant because I thought he was in rehab with several months to go. I met Thomas at a Mexican restaurant within walking distance of my office. I immediately noticed he was fire-eyed, looking a bit frantic. I went to order and Thomas didn't want to eat, just talk, so I ordered for myself and sat at a table to hear what was so important. Thomas began by asking me if I still owned all my guns, which is not your ordinary conversation starter. I told him that yes, I did, and asked him why he would want to know. Thomas went on to tell me that he needed to confess something to me about my guns. Alright then, Thomas had my attention and he leaned forward and whispered the following: "Years ago, I recorded all of the serial numbers of your guns and then I reported them stolen in a home burglary so your guns will come up stolen if the cops ever get a hold of them." Well, over the last few years, I had not only carried these guns from state to state as I moved, I also hunted with them openly and went to shooting ranges, so if I had been carrying stolen guns, I was just a bit pissed off. But I didn't immediately worry because I had developed a drama-of-the-drug-addict filter, and asked him a few questions:

"Why, Thomas? What should I do with the guns if they are hot?"

Thomas immediately insisted that he would pick them up and throw them in a river or someplace where they would never be found! I am not making this up. If this addict thinks I am going to hand over my gun collection, which is always locked in a gun safe, so he can go trade it for a fix, he's hallucinating...well maybe that is true.

So I said, "Why don't I just get rid of the guns?" To which he replied it was too dangerous and he would handle this chore for me as a favor since he caused the problem. By the way, sadly, this is about as close to apologizing as he has ever come for the hell he has put me through over the years.

Thomas insisted until I firmly said, "No. And I have no intention of tossing my guns in the river." Then Thomas started to become angry.

"Fine," he spat, "then you can explain it to the police when they arrest you for possession of stolen property."

I said, "Well, that will be an easy explanation because I'll just ask them who reported my property stolen?"

Thomas became very angry and stormed out of the restaurant.

Shortly after that he called my cell phone a couple of times with some ranting about how he tried to help me and I was in on the original scam of my own guns. I just let the messages go to voice mail, recorded them for my own documentation just in case.

Apparently you don't need to have money to be addicted to money, just like you don't need to have money to have a $1,000 per day drug addiction. You just need to see your goal and step on everything that is good, everyone who loves or trusts you and reach for your brass ring because when you are an addict it is all about you.

Addiction destroys the whole family and for generations.

Chapter 5: Why Kids Start Using—availability, pain, curiosity, rebellion, etc.

A discussion of all of the theories of why kids start using drugs is beyond the scope of this book, but suffice to say, for every kid it can be quite different. (See Figure 4: Some Reasons for Drug Abuse AND Figure 8: Resources with More Information.)

It could be anything from being prescribed a medication for an injury, trying someone else's medication, getting so drunk that they bow to peer pressure and try some substance that ends up making them feel better at the time. Or it could be about their low self esteem, or just trying to fit in with the "cool crowd." Perhaps it is something deeper that drives them to drugs; like molestation by a neighbor or relative, an abusive parent, an unexpected or tragic death or relationship that makes them feel worthless, and they find that they can bury that horrible feeling deep with the drugs they consume.

Brandon had a number of contributing factors, including the death of a friend, a taste for the drug, and a desire not to feel anything.

Stacy, the child prostitute I told you about in Chapter 3, was just fifteen when her parents' divorce, followed by a move to a different state with her mother set in motion a series of events which led her down the path to drug addiction and prostitution, and affected her life forever. Her mother, struggling with and bitter from the divorce, moved them to a new home in suburban El Dorado Hills, California, hundreds of miles away from the life Stacy had known. They had money, and the divorce settlement allowed them to move into a neighborhood filled with well-to-do families. Stacy was confused, hurt, angry, and dealing with a set of circumstances that many teenagers experience without turning to drugs and getting addicted. She had green grass, a large home and a prestigious school, but the sound of her mother's voice became the proverbial fingernails on a chalkboard. Stacy picked up where she left off in Oregon at her new school. She joined the high school dance team, continued with her straight A's, and was a normal young girl from the outside with minimal apparent self-esteem issues. Stacy's self-esteem plummeted when, shortly after her sixteenth birthday, she began experimenting with the drug Ecstasy to fit in with her new friends. Now, it wasn't her school friends that first tempted and provided Stacy with the drug that would soon own her, it was the young people she met at her new synagogue. I just emphasize this so that you see it happens in the most unlikely of places!

"Susan and Troy"

In a beautiful home in an upper class neighborhood, secure inside a gated entryway, my ears heard things I will never forget and my eyes saw things that cannot be erased. I had met this mother after one of my speaking engagements, and I knew how important her story was to my message. I knew the story of her youngest son's addiction didn't end well, but addiction never ends well, and for some the outcome and the ripple into the future is more dramatic than others. I pulled up across from her home as I verified the address on my scribbled paper beside me. I didn't use my iPhone to record this interview like I had with the interview with Stacy, the young lady who told me the chilling story about her journey into teenage prostitution.

I connected with most of the people I have talked to and whose stories I am sharing through phone calls and emails, but toward the end of my writing this book I found myself seeking more private face to face conversations with those so deeply afflicted by addiction. I needed to know more, because I knew a reader would need more proof that addiction does happen to normal everyday people in all walks of life, all ages, shapes, sizes and colors. Addiction crosses all social and economic boundaries, and it doesn't care if you're married, single, gay or straight. No person, no child, is exempt, and yet we parents continue chanting the same tune: "It will not happen to my child."

Addiction is like a landmine that is unsuspectingly stepped on and lives are changed forever. They are changed in so many different ways; the tales have variations. Some who are impacted by the blast may lose a limb, others their hearing, others may lose their life, some will mentally be changed forever, and the effect on friends and family is unimaginable. Like the pieces of a land mine that fly in so many directions, those emotionally and physically damaged may not even be discovered for years to come. Most discover their injury immediately but few know how deeply they are cut.

This home is filled with grief and despair, occupied by a woman who had three sons: Two are living, and one is dead. His presence, however, exists palatably. The mother, who I'm calling Susan, must be in her own living hell.

The blinds are closed and paper is taped across the windows on either side of the front door, and it is dark in the foyer when I arrive. Susan is polite and I dimly recognize her from our brief encounter as I was shaking hands and greeting people after a speech, but I remember what words she quietly shared with me that evening, and those words brought me here. A young man whisks through, telling Susan, "Mom, I'll be back a while later." Susan stops him to introduce me to Steven, her middle child, now her youngest, and I see her parenting skills kick in as she enforces a polite introduction. Steven says a quick hello, but makes little eye contact—he knows why I am here. My presence is yet another reminder of his family tragedy. I can feel him pulling away; he doesn't want to talk to me, and I completely understand, as I am just another grim reminder of a tragedy he wishes he could forget, but I know he never will.

The living room is perfectly decorated, and Susan walks me toward two separate couches that hug the corner of the room. She stops just before we reach the couches and points at the coffee table. "This is him," she says, gesturing towards a decorative box in the center of this table. "This is my youngest son, Troy." She fights her emotions. "I hope it doesn't bother you to sit here next to him." And I quickly say no, it's fine. We sit in the two separate couches but at the end of each making us as close as possible without sitting on the same couch. Troy's ashes are between us.

Susan is obviously uncomfortable even though she has invited me to hear her story but I completely understand the bearing of your soul to help others. This has become my passion and she too wants to help other families learn from her devastation so that another child does not sit silently in an urn. It is a constant reminder of all that went wrong and a call to the second-guessing of herself for what she could have done differently.

"This is a song his friends wrote for the funeral," she says, pointing to lyrics, nicely framed, on the table next to Troy's ashes, and surrounded by ribbons and glitz. Troy had so many friends, and they even signed a banner to him. It is, for all intents and purposes, a shrine to her youngest son. Over 1,000 people attended his funeral, she tells me, with no small sense of pride. Susan's eyes swell with tears, and I assure her that she can share with me whatever she feels comfortable with, and I will leave whenever she wants me to.

"Tell me all you want to tell me about Troy and your family but please tell me when you have shared enough."

Susan begins to open up and starts from the beginning, telling me about her pride in Troy, his accomplishments, his intellect and his addiction. Troy was always a smart kid, he went through some self-esteem issues when he was young and awkward, she states. From where I sit, I can see his graduating class picture: an image of an incredibly handsome young man. What could happen to move that beautiful child from the heights of his accomplishments to the box that lay before me?

I could tell that Susan was one strong, driven lady. She lived in this beautiful home, in this prestigious neighborhood, and she had raised three sons alone and put them through the best schools available. She volunteered for all of their sporting events, and not only did she bring home the bacon, she fried it up in a pan. She was as close to a super-mom as I had met.

Troy's biological dad had been out of the picture since Troy was less than a year old. Disappearing one night never to be seen again, he was a drug addict that straightened up long enough to father three boys, but not long enough to watch his last son blow out the candle on his first birthday cake. Susan had not heard from him since, and when I asked her where he was, she said that she had no clue at all, and that if Troy's father was alive, which she doubted, she knew one thing for sure: Troy's father didn't know his own son was dead. She wasn't bitter about being abandoned; she didn't dwell on that part of her life for one second. Susan was determined to fulfill her children's dreams and aspirations without a man and as a single mom.

Addiction in the family is a very dangerous trait, but having said that, addiction starts somewhere at some time. The propensity to become addicted is statistically stronger the more one's past is darkened with a history of addiction, any addiction.

For Troy, it may have started when, at fifteen, his girlfriend was struck by a drunk driver on a dark road on a night that he was supposed to be with her. A last minute change of plans had sent the young lovers in different directions that evening. Troy never stopped blaming himself for not being there to protect her. He suffered a serious case of survivor guilt, and turned to prescription drugs to make himself stop feeling this self-induced pain. In this affluent neighborhood, they were in almost every medicine cabinet on the block. Friends, relatives, or a random visit to just about any home will yield all the drugs anyone could ever want. Troy's desire not to feel was satisfied by drugs, and because his father was an addict, it can be argued he had a genetic predisposition towards addiction; this wouldn't be helpful when it came time to quit.

Susan noticed Troy's addiction and drug abuse early after the accident. She did everything she should have done and everything I didn't do. She found professional help immediately and sent him off to a rehab center for juveniles. Troy spent several months in treatment, and although Susan had high hopes when Troy returned, the demon of addiction and Troy's darkness crept back into his life. Not long after his return from rehab, she got a call in the middle of the night that Troy had been arrested for driving under the influence—an irony when you consider that his girlfriend died from the same type of driver, but a sign that addiction was taking over and running his life. He spent a few days at the juvenile center because there was an accident involved, and when he came home, went directly to his room and didn't come out at all. He was in a dark, dark place, and he would spend hours in the bathroom, which is a usual spot for addicts to consume and smoke drugs, not just pot, but Oxy and heroin or whatever they can get their hands on.

Steven came home in the afternoon, walked into his own bedroom, and found Troy laying on the ground in the closet below the attic crawl space opening, an orange extension cord tied into a makeshift hangman's noose swaying slowly in the air. Steven instinctively dropped, began CPR and called 911. The medics arrived and were able to resuscitate Troy, who had been fortunate enough to tie the noose the wrong way allowing his body struggling for air to break free. Troy was alive with only minor leg injuries.

Troy needed professional help, and Susan did what she could to make sure he got the best available. After a stay at a mental health facility aimed at getting him past his suicidal thoughts, he began an out-patient program to see him through withdrawals, address his abuse and addiction to a dangerous smorgasbord of drugs. During treatment, Troy confided to his mom that he had been sexually assaulted during his short stint at the juvenile center after his arrest, and he was deeply scarred from the experience. He told her that a female staff member had assaulted him in a room while he was restrained by a straitjacket and bound to a table for acting up and using profanity. As far as Troy was concerned, the worst place in the world was in the custody of police. He was deeply afraid, but that fear was not enough to keep him either off the substances or out from behind the wheel while under the influence.

Just before Troy's eighteenth birthday, he was arrested again for another car accident in which he was under the influence of drugs and alcohol at nearly three times the legal limit. His counselors were contacted, and his family was a wreck. Susan's oldest son, Bobby, who was living away in another state wouldn't even talk to Troy as he heard the horror stories and watched his own mother torn to shreds. Steven was already a complete mess after finding his little brother barely alive, and was completely traumatized. Not only was he sleeping in a bed that faced the closet he found his little brother nearly dead in, Steven was living in a home that was disintegrating before his weary eyes. This family was in complete agony, and everyone was mad at everyone in a home where calm and order once existed. All eyes were on Troy, and as is common with the addict among us, all other siblings feel like their good or normal behavior goes unnoticed as a fire is burning in their midst.

A court appointment was scheduled, and Susan drove a terrified Troy to his hearing for the latest driving-under-the-influence charge. As Susan approached the court, Troy became increasingly panicked. Troy was losing control and talking about killing himself; he couldn't contemplate returning to juvenile hall. Susan was trying to drive and calm him as she pulled into the courthouse parking lot. As soon as the car came to a stop, Troy leapt from the vehicle, darting like a wild animal through the lot and had disappeared within a few moments. Susan was frantic and tried to get the officers inside the court to help her retrieve him. Susan pleaded with them, telling them Troy had threatened to kill himself and had already tried once. The officers told Susan there was nothing they could do, as Troy hadn't caused any problems inside the court and they hadn't seen him bolt.

Susan returned to her car defeated and sat there wondering what would happen when Troy didn't show for his scheduled court appointment, when suddenly Troy walked up to her in the lot. Susan was shocked that Troy had returned, and she knew they still had time to make the appearance at the hearing. Troy seemed calm and his demeanor was different; he was ready to walk into the court and appear for his case. My personal thought is that Troy took drugs to calm himself, but I honestly have no evidence of that except for my experience with addicts. If Troy didn't want to feel, he knew exactly how to accomplish that.

The judge listened to all of Troy's charges and calmly ruled that Troy would be charged as an adult with a felony for both the accident and the driving under the influence of drugs and alcohol. With the impact of the gavel, Troy's mood began to devolve. Once he and Susan were outside, Troy exploded and said that he wasn't going to prison, he wasn't going to be tried as an adult, and he wasn't going to be raped in prison by some animal. Susan's goal was to get Troy home and calm him down, but she was very afraid. She managed to get a call off to his doctor, texting him the numbers "9-1-1" before Troy slapped the phone from her hand. Somehow the text went through.

They were within a short distance of home when she had to stop at a red traffic light. As soon as the car stopped, Troy threw his door open and ran wildly down the street. Susan had no way to catch him and no way to know where he had gone. She called Steven at home, and Steven called 911. Susan was so exhausted when she arrived home that she felt like she was having a heart attack, but all she worried about was Troy, where he was, what he had done, whether he was dead or alive and how could this mother save her son from what she instinctively felt was his darkest moment.

The paramedics arrived, responding to the 911 call, and immediately took control of Susan. Her blood pressure was off the charts, but she begged them to leave her alone and find Troy. Steven was there the whole time watching as this disaster just seemed to grow by the second. The paramedics insisted that they needed to take Susan to the hospital immediately. Steven followed the ambulance to the hospital while Susan was strapped to a gurney shouting that her son will kill himself if she leaves. She was given a sedative. Steven got Troy to answer his cell phone, told him the condition of their mother and that they were headed to the hospital. Steven was in shock and frantic to keep up with the ambulance, and he told Troy one final thing before he hung up: "You know what you need to do."

Susan awakened from her sedative in the hospital frantic; she sat up to see Steven in the room and made one statement to Steven: "Troy is dead!" Susan got out of the hospital bed and told Steven to drive her home, now, and he obeyed, trancelike.

When they pulled up in front of their home and Susan said to him, "I can't go in, I just can't," Steven walked in through the garage, through the house, searching for any sign of his little brother. He walked from room to room and saw nothing until he reached the last room, his own room. There, he noticed something out of place: a pair of shoes with socks lying on top in the doorway. He looked in and called Troy's name but there was no answer. Steven walked further in the room and saw a stack of his clothes and jackets from his closet neatly placed in a corner. This time, his little brother had tied the noose correctly.

CPR. 911. Paramedics. Susan remained in the car, knowing, in her broken heart, that Steven had been gone too long and certain that her youngest child was dead. Steven was exhausted by his failed effort to save his brother. Just as a mother's intuition knew the day he was born that he was coming into this world, Susan was just as certain of the last day of her son's life.

"I can't bury him or put him anywhere, so I have him here with me," she sobbed to me, "I just don't want Troy to be alone, so when I die I want him buried with me."

I leaned forward and placed my hand on her shoulder; I was extremely affected.

"His nineteenth birthday is coming up, and in another month it will be a year since Troy died."

I began to weep with her. I could never know the actual pain she felt because she had buried her eighteen-year old son less than a year ago. Pictures of her three boys were everywhere and Troy was in almost every one. "He spoke three languages, he got straight A's, he played three sports, he had everything going for him until one night when the phone rang with the news that the young girl he loved was dead."

Susan stopped talking, and she looked at me with kindness and relief that she had been able to share the story of her son with me to help others understand that addiction kills in different ways than an overdose. "Would you like to see Troy's room? I haven't touched anything... This is his bed; Troy made it that morning and I haven't changed the sheets. His dog sleeps in here on the floor next to his bed." She pointed toward the floor. "His dog used to get in bed with him but she won't get up there anymore; she waits for him here and it's been eleven months." She pulled the sleeve of his high school letterman jacket out from between the clothes that hung in the closet. She was proud of her boy and she missed him and she knew the family she had worked so hard to build as a single mom was in tatters.

"Do you want to see where he hung himself?"

I said, "Whatever you want to show me, I'm fine." In reality, I'm stunned!

Susan took me by the hand and guided me to the room next door. It had been Steven's room, but after Troy died there, Steven moved into his older brother, Bobby's room. We entered this room and she slid the closet door open and pointed up to the attic crawl space door. Susan said, "I need to get this painted up there because you can still see the marks from the cord on the sheetrock when his body was trying to survive." I looked up and you could clearly see the marks, they were visible and so were the kick marks against the wall as the natural instinct of his body was to kick, squirm and convulse as it strived for another breath. "I can't paint it because the only ladder I have is the one he used. I need to get a new ladder," she muttered. Paint might cover these marks, but nothing was ever going to cover the scars left on this family just as nothing was going to bring this son, brother, and friend, back.

Addiction and drugs alter these young minds convincing them there is no tomorrow and when the drugs wouldn't stop the demons that controlled Troy, he stopped his life. He had no thought of a better day ahead. He couldn't see the mayhem he would leave in the wake of his actions, the emotional toll that this would take on his family. Troy couldn't comprehend that a young man might grow to one day be a husband, an uncle, a father and that he could have had years of laughter and happiness ahead of him. He couldn't imagine tomorrow. He was an eighteen-year old who felt nothing but hopelessness; a child to a mother, a grandchild and brother, and he left behind only the haunted souls of the people who loved him.

By telling that story, I don't mean to suggest that there is always a deep emotional wound that leads to drug use. There can be no reason other than just wanting to fit in with a group, being afraid to lose the peer group that is so important to adolescents—it might be the way they self-identify. But the funny thing about friendships between addicts is that they are based on a common preference for drugs—when the chips are down, these are not friends. These so-called friends will scatter like rats when a true friend is needed more than ever, when all that needs to happen is that a passed out drunk be rolled over, or that someone who has overdone it be brought to the attention of their parents, or that when someone is overdosing they be brought to the hospital that a 911 call be made.

I have held a father who lost his son—he was dumped in a highway median in the gravel while overdosing. The coroner said he lived for several hours and would have likely survived if his fellow drug-addicted "friends" had dropped him at one of the several hospitals they had driven past because they simply didn't want to get caught.

Another mother I talked to came downstairs as she woke in the morning to find her son sleeping on the couch where she had last seen him with some friends watching a movie the night before. A closer look at him, because his position seemed odd and he had no blanket covering him, revealed that he was cold, blue, and dead from an overdose. The friends would later say they thought he just passed out after they shared some prescription meds for fun.

Some Reasons for Drug Abuse

Abandonment by a parent

Survivor guilt

Tragedy

Desire not to feel pain: physical or emotional

Desire to fit in with a crowd

Rebellion

Adolescent feelings of invulnerability

Low self esteem

Easy access

Belief prescriptions are "safe"

Figure 4

"Martha"

I met one mom in my meetings and her story chilled me to the bone. That is saying something. I'll call this mother "Martha." Martha knew her daughter was spinning out of control and hoped for better days. Her daughter was of adult age, and Martha could only watch in horror, as we did for so many years with our son, as addiction controlled her daughter's every move. The doorbell rang late in the night but just once awaking both Martha and her husband. They listened for a second ring and collectively dismissed it as a prank. Morning came, coffee was started, and she set off towards the front door to fetch the newspaper from the porch. Upon opening the door the lifeless body of her daughter sat against the doorframe, slightly tilting in as the door swung open. Overdosing and a threat to her friends, they decided to drop her home, ring the doorbell and run to safety. This mother will never forget the sight of her dead daughter on the porch. Fellow drug abusers are not friends.

Whatever the reason that one kid decides to abuse drugs, whatever the contributing factors are, once they cross that bridge they have begun a trip down a very, very dangerous road, and because of the changing nature of drugs, it is harder to turn around.

Chapter 6: Signs and symptoms

What are the signs and symptoms of prescription drug abuse? I thought I'd know. I didn't.

Listing all the signs and symptoms of drug experimentation and abuse are beyond the scope of this book and readily available elsewhere, not to mention that the drugs abused today are not the same as those abused in my teenage years and they will likely change for every generation to come. Of course, we've got the subtle signs that we might ignore or chalk up to "normal" adolescence: Moodiness, loss of interest in school and other activities, problems with academics. And then we've got other signs that we might ignore or chalk up to "normal" rebellious behavior, such as: cigarette smoking, group affiliation and clothing choices, idolizing figures from the drug subculture. Then we've got obvious signs that we should not under any circumstances ignore. And it's with these that I'd like to spend a bit of time.

As much as I am asked or I hear others asked what the signs of addiction are, they are just so abundant and easily dismissed that it is a difficult question to address. (See Figure 6: Signs of drug abuse)

Brandon always had a constant parade of new friends walking into our home, while the previous friends would vanish as quickly as they appeared. These friends were not necessarily friendly, usually keeping conversations and eye contact to a minimum. They also kept their distance as if they didn't want you close enough to touch them or smell them or see their dilated or red eyes. I couldn't commit Brandon's friends' names to memory, with rare exception.

Brandon suddenly had zero interest in sports; even though he was a great football player in his freshman and sophomore year, he now "hated" it. His grades were dropping like flies, and according to him, were always the fault of some horrible teacher who "hated him." Be careful: Your child will set you up to hate the people who are most likely to out them as addicts, including teachers, counselors and the police.

As I tell you these signs, I want you to understand that these signs mirror those shared with me by the parents of hundreds of other addicts and they all had one common thread and that was drama! Nothing came with a simple explanation. Drug abusers always have a dramatic flair: Agitation was present almost anytime we had a family event or social gathering that required his attendance.

Brandon had lost interest in our hot rod project—rebuilding our 1967 Chevy Chevelle. Once his dream car, pictures of the Chevelle still adorned his wall and his screen saver on his cell phone was a picture of the Chevelle. He still bragged wildly about the Chevelle in a nearly delusional way to his friends (but good luck to me when I needed his help working on it). The Chevelle became a grim symbol of the person he was becoming. I could hardly walk past the Chevelle and look straight at it. I began to avoid looking at a car!

Brandon's lying to us had become the rule rather than the exception and his lies were so blatantly unbelievable that it was an insult that he thought we would believe these tall tales. It was as if he thought we were the stupidest people on earth. He would tell these lies to other family and friends as well. He was late to every dinner, began to "hate" foods he had always eaten so he would sometimes barely touch his meal. He was late to parties and family events and his excuses for his tardiness or failure to show up at all were increasingly ludicrous. Addicts are usually late to family events because they are on drugs and paranoid that they will be noticed as high. He was gaunt and his complexion suffered with acne but we quickly chalked that up to those typical teenage years. For the most part we could easily justify his appearance because we simply and deeply didn't want to face the facts that would lead us to the truth that Brandon had a serious addiction.

Even if one parent is savvy, the addict will exploit the weaker parent and the survival of your marriage does not factor in to their manipulating you, in fact it helps the addicts if you are at odds with your spouse. Stepparents usually see the addiction long before a biological parent and we know that the addict will paint the stepparent as evil to facilitate their ability to continue their addiction. They will move in with Grandpa when they have exhausted you and they won't leave there until they are thrown out, usually after all of Grandma's medications turn up missing.

Just as your children lie to you and con you in every way they can to get drugs, and just like they divide and conquer mom and dad, they will build a wall between you and the police. Another sign of drug use is trouble with the cops, and obviously, getting caught red handed. It's not your child's drugs the cop found in Johnny's pocket, those weren't even his pants! It is that absurd. Have you ever watched an episode of "Cops"? It's never the driver's drugs or guns in the car he is driving, somebody else must have put them there. Your addict might have multiple traffic tickets and car accidents, but it's never their fault.

All of these signs and symptoms add up to the one conclusion that we do not want to face so we excuse all of them. We assist our children in becoming more deeply addicted by revealing to them how gullible we are and how easy we are to lie to.

Some signs of possible drug abuse		
moodiness	loss of interest in activities	problems with academics
excessively long time in the bathroom	unfriendly peers who avoid eye contact	conspiracy stories
dramatic explanations	agitation	tardiness to family activities
loss of appetite	gaunt/pale coloring	black fingertips/smudges on doors/clothes
trouble with police	not accepting responsibility	evasive eye contact
quick trips to grab something from the house or car	friends who wait in the car	missing valuables
new valuables of unexplained origin	requests to see the doctor for pain	ID cards with worn out edges or powder residue
insolent behavior	paraphernalia: missing spoons, broken ball point pens	etc.

Figure 5

Additional signs that Brandon and his associates/friends were using drugs all seem as clear as the nose on my face now: Little or evasive eye contact, constant trips to the bathroom (addicts smoke/consume/inject drugs in private spots), quick trips outside to the car, friends waiting in the car while Brandon quickly ran in to our home to get something or change shoes or some lame excuse (so he could snatch his stash from its hiding place). Drug addicts don't trust addicts with their stash, period! If they have drugs hidden, they are nearby and usually somewhere in their bedroom or their car, in a nook or a cranny—if you want to find them, look very close at everything from a compact disc cover to the pockets of pants or shirts that hang in the closet.

His drastic clothing changes from semi-normal teenager to gangster sweat suits and hats worn sideways we chalked up to a rebellious young adult, but were actually much more than that. He wore oversized baggy clothing in an attempt to mask his deteriorating body, long sleeve shirts and sweaters that covered his arms, even when it was tee-shirt weather. More common signs I saw and hear from other parents include a lack of personal hygiene, a total lack of upkeep on personal belongings and his vehicle; the trophies and trinkets your children once cherished will be dropped in some corner or broken and left where they lie. This is an easy one to spot and it truly translates into them suddenly not caring about their things because the sole focus of their life is drugs—where they will get them, how they will pay for them, and where and when they will consume them. This is a full time obsession! God forbid we left our keys out as our son would take the car out, leave trash in it, the stereo blaring rap music and the driver's seat in the low rider position, all without a thought that we might notice. Always remember that an addict's attention is 100% on their drugs so they get sloppy and leave obvious signs. Plus, they are convinced you are clueless, as you have proven to them that you are.

There may be random injuries that require a trip to the doctor and they might complain about their doctor and request a new doctor (otherwise known as "Rx hunting" or "doctor shopping"). They may request to see a specific doctor that a friend of them is seeing as they know this doctor is quick with the Rx pad. Dirty doctors are out there, and they prey on your children as they line their pockets with your cash. Search the name of doctors on the internet and you just may discover that other parents have reported that this doc is dirty!

Other common signs include: The ability to suddenly afford clothing that is trendy and expensive, a sudden collection of valuables such as cameras, TV's, computers and other miscellaneous items that can be traded for drugs and are likely stolen from other parents by their own addicted children (this is also a sign that your child is dealing drugs). Or, they have suddenly lost their valuables like cameras and sporting equipment (or you are missing valuables...where did I leave that watch?)—they have hocked them or traded them for drugs. When you find yourself hiding your purse and wallet and locking up valuables but you will not admit your child may have a drug problem, you are in denial, and your child is in danger!

If you see blood spots on clothing near the arms and down to the sleeves (drug addicts who inject do not use a Band-Aid or cotton ball and tape), trouble sleeping with almost a complete shift to sleeping during the day and up at night (of course, they tell you they can't sleep and they want to see a doctor for this because you will drive them to get the drugs they will abuse), long showers behind locked doors (to hide the smell of burning drugs), missing foil, burned odd items found in the garage or trash (check your trash cans, especially in the bathroom the child uses), signs that the screen on your child's bedroom window is being opened regularly, calloused and soot-coated fingers from burning drugs like Oxy and Heroin on foil so intently that they don't care or feel the pain of their own skin burning, water bottles filled with vodka in their backpack, credit or ID cards that are worn out on the edges from chopping snort-able drugs (wipe your finger along the edges of plastic cards and when powder appears, you have a problem), a complete lack of respect for you as a parent, quick short stops to "get something" in some place you can't see them means they have stashed a drug at your home, broken writing pens with the outer part of the pen missing (used as a stem pipe and usually shortened to half the size of the normal pen casing). Missing spoons from your silverware drawer are a strong sign somebody is injecting something (all forks, knives and no spoons might mean you have a child injecting drugs).

Check receipts and the contents of their wallet, pockets or purse. If there is an ATM receipt from the other side of town and they swear they were a block away all night, they scored drugs somewhere. Addicts are so focused on their next fix that they will get very sloppy and leave obvious signs if you will just pry your hands away from your eyes!

The presence of paraphernalia is a sure sign. I met a woman on a flight to LA and we got talking about our kids. Her son is seventeen years old, and well, long story short, she didn't have any clue about the signs of Rx drug abuse. Missing aluminum foil? Pens without their plastic shell? This mom had experienced both! So I gave her a copy of *Defining Moments*. A week later, I received an email:

> *It was a pleasure to meet you and even more of a pleasure to read your book. I got so wrapped up in the book that I was getting irritated that I kept getting interrupted and I had to put the book down. I read the book on a business trip. I couldn't wait to get home and toss out all my old medications. That was first on my list. The second thing I did was go through my 17 years old's CD covers and video game cassettes. I was happy not to find anything!*
>
> *My son and I had a long talk about drugs in general. I gave him your book to read. We watched the video of your son going through withdrawals together. He couldn't watch it but he saw enough to get the message. Thank you for telling your story and opening my eyes. EVERY parent needs to read your book.*

The list of signs goes on and on. I know any reasonable person would surmise that only a complete idiot (me in this case) would ignore all of these signs, and I agree; but consider that these scenarios, symptoms, and signs occur over many years. I also return to the fact that it is always easy to make the correct call from the cheap seats while we parents sit in the front row and ignore reality.

We parents evolve into enabling over the life of a child and all the way into our offspring's adult years. No ice cream for little Johnny and that's final...five minutes later, Johnny has a chocolate covered face. It happens; we give in to the child's demands at all ages all the way up to the point of no return. We defend our children like a lion defends her cub, and that defense can cause us to look away from obvious signs of addiction that could change the rest of everyone's life unless they are addressed ASAP! A parent just doesn't know or simply can't stop parenting, and at some point, with a drug abuser, parenting becomes enabling. We are enabling our children to death.

Chapter 7: Where parents start to mess up. Enabling behaviors.

Mistake #1: Accepting Experimentation

Some parents think it is alright if their child is experimenting with alcohol or marijuana, but I believe that they are dead wrong. I know I tried it and I am fine, perhaps you tried it and you are fine, but all the rules have changed. Thanks to hybridization, marijuana really is up to twenty times stronger than what we fooled around with. Put that little thought in perspective: You smoked a joint with a friend in 1980 and you were fine, maybe a little giggly or dizzy, and now your child smokes a joint with his friend and your child's share of splitting one joint is roughly equivalent to you smoking ten to twenty joints in 1980. Are you still okay with this experimentation? Smoking ten joints was a huge tolerance for someone "back in the day" and was almost unthinkable. Think of what inhaling the equivalent to ten joints in THC might do to your inhibitions about trying the next drug in line after the gate is open—perhaps a pill that will make your head stop spinning and settle you down. Letting this "natural adolescent experimentation" slide is playing with fire, and if you dismiss this as normal behavior for your child, you are putting that child among peers who have access to every other drug. Maybe they will prefer the pill, and because parents are not as likely to observe the signs of prescription drug usage, as they would smell reeking clothes or see squinty red eyes, they may find the pill a more discreet option. Plus, the pill bottle has your doctor's name on it, so there is a false sense of security.

Even parents might accept experimentation thinking somehow, like their kids do, that if a medicine is prescribed by a doctor, it is somehow safer. Medical cannabis distribution is legal here in California and in several other states, leading some adolescents and adults to believe that heck—smoking a little dope might even be good for you. It follows that prescription drugs might lend themselves to that same perception. If the drugs your child obtains have your doctor's name on the label they must be safe, right? Parents mustn't accept the argument that just because a drug comes legally with a prescription that it is not a dangerous substance.

Many signs or symptoms of drug abuse can be easily dismissed as the actions of a teenager who is morphing into an adult, no longer your child, and naturally distancing themselves from you, their parent, but it doesn't pay to keep our heads in the sand.

I hope your child is right that they will never get addicted if they experiment with drugs. Experimenting is Russian roulette and you may not blow your brains out on the first few spins, but the odds start to look dim as you continue to pull the trigger. I hope you are among the few who have perfect children that never ever take the chance of becoming addicted, but are you willing to just strap on your blinders and hope for the best? Some children play with fire and don't get burned, some burn to death.

I've said it before without much popularity with the parents of younger children: "There are two types of kids in the world, those who smoke pot and those who are going to try it." I do believe that children will smoke pot, drink booze, and try drugs. I do believe some will consider it an experience in their life and move on to more productive lives. I did it, and I know many who took the correct path after teenage experimentation. But you can't just count on your kids following your footsteps. As I've said before and I'll say again, pot is so much stronger that it is dangerous to compare it to what we experienced in the 60's, 70's and 80's. Also we did not look in the medicine cabinet and find synthetic heroin under the guise of a prescription from a doctor and share it at the teenage party. This is jumping off the bridge and we and our children have no clue how truly strong and addictive these easily accessible legal drugs are. Some children do not live past the first pill they try.

Mistake #2: Believing Everything the Kids Say, Despite Evidence

Don't be fooled, look at them with fresh eyes—as if you are not related—and examine their behavior. A parent who wants to assume the best will want to believe that it's not that bad, but try to step back and see from a position of strength as a person who truly wants to know what is really going on in the life of this child.

It's not easy to look at your child objectively when they have grown up with you, and, compounding the issue is that they have also mastered manipulating you from an early age. You are not "bullshit proof," in fact, you are very vulnerable to your own child's deceit. You have been coddling them their whole life. They have honed their manipulation of you and perfected their skills over time. You have become the enabler of their wants and desires because you love them and you want them to be happy. They know it, and they may know you better than you know yourself! If they want to hide something from you, they can, and if they are addicted to drugs, they will.

If you catch them with one pill, it's not theirs. If you catch them taking a pill it was the first time. If you catch them with a bag of pot or a bottle of pills, they were just holding it for someone else who will kill them if they don't return it. The lies are countless and you will believe whatever you want if you can't or won't face the truth. The truth is, dismiss any of these lies and you may join the ranks of those of us who have lived the hell of addiction. The club of "not my child" grows every time a parent accepts a complete and total line of bullshit because that parent doesn't really want to know the truth, or looks past that telling moment because they are just too busy to look close enough to be led to the clues that may lead to an undesirable conclusion. We need to look at our own kids as critically as we are inclined to judge others.

This is really, really hard. Parents I talk to are disbelieving. Just because my kid was a lying addict doesn't mean that their kid is. They believe that their child's problem can't be as bad as my Brandon's was. They believe I'm just bitter because it happened to me, and I want to bring down the rest of the room because my kid was a fuck up. They believe their children have never lied to them and never would—I understand why parents feel the need to believe this. I hope they are right. But please recognize that drugs change a child. Your child is gone once he or she is an addict and is replaced by a replica of your child who will look you straight in the face and lie about everything that was sacred in your relationship. You stand between them and a drug which now owns them. An addict can justify every despicable action if it gets them to the target, the drug; this is their new relationship.

Mistake #3 and #4: Denial and Believing Staying Ignorant will Make it Go Away

"Billy's Parents"

A husband and wife called me while I was on one of my writing escapes to Capitola, CA. I still take every call, and I am happy to be that shoulder to cry on when a family discovers that they have an addict among them or in this case "a freshman away at college who is experimenting with drugs." This particular call was one of the most unbelievable examples of denial I have ever experienced. Mom and Dad were both on the phone with me, and the mother was dominant. I get all types but when one parent does most of the talking, I consider that they are the dominant of the two parents, and usually the most gullible. If I could speak in general terms, and after hundreds of calls and conversations I believe I have earned my wings to do so, I find with married couples who call about addiction of their child, the dad speaks more if they are calling about a daughter and the mom speaks more if they are calling about a son. The opposite sex parent is also more likely to defend or deny the reality of the situation for that child while the same sex parent is more likely to start to agree with me when I call "bullshit."

Back to this particular call, Mom proceeds to tell me that they are very concerned that their son, Billy, has begun experimenting with drugs since he went to college just a few months before. Mom then tells me that they just received their second call from the hospital in as many months. I ask, "The hospital?" because I thought she had just told me he had begun experimenting and usually I don't get "experimenting" and "hospital" in the same call. Mom continues, telling me they think he might have a drug problem.

I ask, "What is he in the hospital for?"

Mom explains, with an occasional "yep" or "uh-uh" from Dad on the other phone, that Billy is hospitalized for his second overdose of heroin in the last two months. Mom goes on to tell me that he has only tried heroin twice (as in these two overdoses) and he has never tried any other drugs!

I have heard my share of denial but we may have a winner here. I said, "How did he take the heroin when he overdosed?"

Mom answers, "Billy injected it with a needle; Why? Is there another way to take it?"

I said to them, "Do you truly believe your son has

experimented with heroin only twice and rolled up his sleeve to shoot heroin in his veins to see how it would feel for his first drug experiment?"

To which she answered, "Yes," followed by her husband's meek, "Yes...I think," followed by the mom's question, "Why do you ask," followed by a barely audible Dad saying, "Yeah, why?"

Well, we are on my time, and they did call me, so as you may have gathered, I tell it like it is. I say, "So, the first time he tried the heroin, it worked out so well with an overdose that he gave it another go?" Come on, people, you don't decide to learn to swim by jumping off the Golden Gate Bridge.

Mom says, "I guess" and Dad, the bubble slowly bursting over his head, says, "Well, maybe not." Mom is not very pleased with Dad's input, so I get to listen to their exchange and dad starts to back down.

I interrupted and told the mom to take the phone into the kitchen. She resisted and didn't understand what I was asking her to do. "Just go to the kitchen and open the silverware drawer; where you keep the flatware," I said.

"Okay," she said, after a brief pause. "I'm here but I really..."

"Is the drawer open?"

"Yes."

"Where are all your spoons?"

After several seconds of silence, she said, "How did you know all my spoons were gone?"

I was feeling impatient and, yes, a bit angry, and I said, "Do you people really want to know what I think?" When they both meagerly said yes, I let them know exactly what I thought. It may not be accurate or correct but they asked my opinion and they were going to receive it.

"I think your son was likely experimenting with prescription drugs long before he went away to college, probably prescriptions located in your medicine cabinet or one nearby, and your son has slowly over time developed an opiate addiction and now that he is far from your medicine cabinet, your son has turned to the cheapest, easily available opiate on the streets and that is heroin."

Heroin is very unpredictable as to potency, unlike a pill made from a pharmaceutical company, so overdoses on heroin are very common for addicts switching from pills to heroin. "Your son is an addict," I told them, "and he needs professional help, and you are lucky he survived two overdoses. You need to pluck his ass out of college and get him in the best rehab center you can afford and thank your lucky stars that you are calling me instead of a funeral director!"

The husband spoke firmly to his wife, who was, at last, speechless: "Honey, we are getting on a plane tomorrow to pick Billy up and we have a lot of calls to make to find him rehab so we need to thank this gentleman for his time and get to work on our plans!"

Although I know Mom and Dad were both in shock, as is any parent when they figure out addiction is real and it has happened to them, I do think they were thankful for my candor. Or she thought I was a magician with a disappearing spoon trick (as I mentioned earlier, spoons are used in the liquefying process). I truly believe that not only will they put their son in rehab, they will get their collective head out of the sand of denial and begin to educate themselves about addiction and become aware of something that they never, ever imagined they would need to understand. The reality has slapped them across the face. And that hurts. Bad.

Addiction may start in many different and even innocent ways but when addiction owns your child's soul, you are in uncharted territory, and you are in these rocky waters because you just couldn't stop being a parent and see the actions of your child as the signs of addiction they were. You would have taken notice of their bizarre behavior, and you would not have searched for justification if this was someone else's child. I assure you if they were your niece or nephew, neighbor or your friend's kid, you would have had them drawn and quartered long ago.

Mistake #5: Distrusting the Police

Your drug experimenting or addicted children need to convince you that the police just want to harass them, to bust them and pin things on them; they are always the victim because a day will come when you will get a knock on the door inquiring about your little Johnny or Janie and you will likely start by lying for or defending your little angel because the groundwork has been set by your addict.

I get it, you don't want your child to go to jail, that is just instinct, but what are you willing to do to stop it? I know, I know, I went undercover and risked my life to save my son's ass from iron bars, small cells, steel toilets and an unknown criminal for a roommate, so I did do everything to save him because I thought that was what a dad should do. You and I can't imagine our children in orange jumpsuits with an inmate number stenciled across their back. The hundreds of parents I talk to are scared to death of the police because they afraid the police are going to haul their little addict away.

Odds are, if your child is using, buying, consuming, selling and/or addicted to drugs, the cops already know who he/she is and they just might know a lot more about your child than you do. They know you too—they know that you will defend your child to the end. They have a thankless job when they knock on your door or arrest your child. But the truth is, for many addicts, this event may bring them closer to their bottom—or their moment of epiphany, as some say—and closer to accepting treatment.

The point is that you will believe your child over anyone and anything, no matter the proof, and all the while you are doing one thing so very well: You are enabling your child to become further addicted to drugs and you are assisting them down the path with your denial closer to the edge of the cliff they are marching off.

Mistake #6: Believing it Can't Happen to Your Family

You might think you are too smart. You might think your child is too smart. You might think your family is too privileged. They play sports, they are the prom queen, yadda, yadda, yadda. But it's important to know that the epidemic of prescription drug abuse was first uncovered in the poverty stricken hills of Appalachia, in economically depressed small towns where entire families were being decimated by prescription drug overdoses. Now, this epidemic is in the wealthiest most economically privileged coastal towns of Southern California. Why would anyone at either end of the spectrum or anywhere in between feel immune?

I'm not a cynic; I am the parent of a recovering drug addict, a husband and father of a recovering family, and I spent most of my life surrounded by lying, hurtful addicts. I see clearly so many of the mistakes I made and I know with certainty that more mistakes lie in wait for me long into my future. I will know exactly what those future mistakes are—sometime after I make them.

The easiest mistakes for us to see are the ones made by another child, family, friend or acquaintance. But my child is a good kid, not like that child over there. Aren't we all experts, sitting comfortably in our chairs looking out our window, across the picket fence as we discuss the easy solutions of those we criticize and judge, all while the walls of our own home quietly crumble around us? Trust me, the neighbor is looking at your predicament in shock at the very same time they ignore their own.

Check up on your kids, even if they're "good." They are going to the synagogue for a youth group? Get names and numbers and check them. That's what Stacy, the addicted prostitute, told her mom. Good student, off to study The Bible? You better check on that. Watch your kids like hawks. Drug test them. Talk to them. Because it can happen to you.

"The instant out" is something a lot of addicts, like Stacy, shared with me. It is a short sentence that they know the parent will buy and it gets them out of the home in seconds to go do what they want to do. Perhaps they always go to a certain friend's home, a gathering like band practice, a study group or something you will say yes to without hesitation and without thought of checking on the validity. Your kids have your number and you need to stop yourself occasionally and let your kids know that you will check up on them. And you need to do it.

Teen-proof your home! We childproofed our home when our children were babies and we watched them like hawks at homes where safety devices were not installed. We need to do the same thing with our older kids, but instead of clamping down the toilet seat and locking the cleansers, we need to educate our parents and neighbors that it is not okay to leave prescriptions out any more than it is okay to leave a loaded gun on the counter. Lock your booze, lock your meds! Dole out your child's prescriptions to them. In the end I am saying that it's better to be prepared and try to prevent disaster than be caught off guard and have to pick up the pieces.

There is an increase in prescription writing in the US coinciding with an increase in marketing and the increased identification of syndromes that can be treated with drugs that can be abused. This is true of painkillers, but also other meds. If a child has a prescription for Ritalin, because little Johnny says he can't pay attention—when I was younger I got a smack on the back of the head with stern instructions to pay attention—he has access to these meds for himself to abuse and also to sell to other students at test time or trade them for stronger drugs other kids harvest from their family medicine cabinet. Little Johnny lost his ADD meds again? You swear he'd lose his head if it wasn't attached! Now you figure you need to call the doctor and get him some more. Parents, wake up! Johnny may be selling, trading and possibly abusing powerful prescription drugs and you are not only enabling him to continue doing so, you are his supplier and you foot the co-pay! If your child is on prescription medication, dole it out to them one by one—never give them the bottle!

Addiction has no socioeconomic boundaries, and your biggest mistake will be thinking that you and your family are immune to addiction because you drive a fancy car to a beautiful home behind a gate code entry. Prescription drug addiction is more common in the very places I describe as these are the homes with cellars full of wine, back-up bottles of name brand highbrow booze and medicine cabinets filled with anything you ask your doctor to prescribe for you or your children.

"Trevor's Family"

Building the moat around your castle—becoming a prisoner in your own home

Parents who live with an active addict in their home live every day in a way they never imagined. I have personally met many families in this situation, but "Trevor's" family is one that is representative of so many other stories of other families. Trevor's addiction grew over time and the family had looked away, hoped it was mostly in their imagination and that it would just get better. Looking back, they now see they should not have ignored or downplayed the earlier signs and symptoms; they see this as clear as they now see the track marks on their child's arms. As with many of the families I have talked to, this child was raised in a prosperous family, a beautiful home, the best school, and was injecting heroin before he was seventeen years old after starting with prescription drugs from the medicine cabinet. He had been sent to rehab several times only to relapse almost immediately every time. Recently assigned to probation, Trevor is "in the system," and still lives at home with his parents.

The step-mother of now eighteen-year old Trevor, a woman who I'll call "Theresa," told me a bit of her predicament and invited me to their house to meet with her family to learn more. Trevor began to spin out of control early in his teens, she said. He was a rebellious young boy who wanted for nothing and soon had a $300 per day heroin habit.

Sure, their friends and family have told them to kick the "loser" kid out, but this is her husband's son and her step-son. Sure her friends have prodded her to leave her husband if he won't "control HIS kid" but the advice from the cheap seats is always easy for those doling it out. As they say, opinions are like assholes, everybody has one. The fact is that she loves her husband "Jason" very much, and they have been living in this hell for several years in hopes of better days and they cling to that. It takes a while to realize exactly how you have adapted your lives to protect yourself from your children and their associates.

I appreciated the invitation, and found myself standing inside the foyer of their beautiful home in a gated community in the San Francisco Bay Area. Barking little dogs were nipping at my ankles as I entered. They were actually real ankle biters, but I didn't mind as I have a couple of those knuckleheads myself. We proceeded to the large kitchen island. The plan was that I would meet all three of them, Theresa, Jason, and Trevor. This was the plan, but I was betting my last dime that the addict would be a no-show. You see, addicts don't like the sound of another person coming to their home to talk to them about addiction, it smells of an intervention and the likelihood of someone throwing a gunny sack over them and dragging them off to some remote rehab center. The fact is that if this had been an intervention, you're never going to give the addict a warning; but try to convince a paranoid drug addict of this fact. Jason thanked me profusely for taking the time to come by and visit with them and assured me that Trevor would be home shortly, but I knew better.

"Why don't we get started and just talk for a while," I suggested, and so the conversation began. Theresa watched her husband's every word as if she was about to learn how he felt for the first time. It was evident that the lines of communication had broken down, as is often the case, and Theresa had earlier shared with me that she and Jason hadn't really been talking for the last week, which was when Trevor was released from jail after a probation violation of testing dirty for marijuana the month before.

Trevor was on juvenile probation after being busted selling almost an ounce of heroin and then subsequently selling pain pills to an undercover officer right in front of this home (he had been set up by a "friend"). A pack of marked and unmarked law enforcement vehicles swarmed into this pristine neighborhood, officers rushed into this fine home—bursting through the door and throwing Trevor on the floor before dragging his handcuffed body to a waiting squad car for all the neighbors to watch. These parents knew deep inside that they are judged and the home they worked so hard for, their castle, is now marred by a black cloud that floats above it. The police retrieved the marked bills and went to court armed with a crisp recording of the drug deal itself and the phone calls leading up to it.

Trevor, who was now being treated for heroin withdrawals with another drug, Subutex, was smoking his Subutex instead of taking it orally as prescribed—in other words, abusing these drugs another reason that I believe that it makes little sense to treat what began as prescription drug addiction with another prescription. Mentally, the addict always thinks they can abuse the drugs they desire and get better later with another pill. Or they buy time with the prescribed drugs to keep withdrawals at bay and then trade their meds for what they really desire. I'm sure Big Pharma would disagree with me, but I'm just saying it doesn't make much sense in my mind.

Trevor's two wonderful law abiding parents have experienced the most bizarre and horrifying events as a result of the Trevor's dealings: Everything from being subjected to humiliating experiences like the one described above, to being robbed, to something that blows my mind. Do you remember the ankle bitters I told you about? They are two six pound dogs that are the love of their lives, as so many of us know what an animal can mean to us. (I always tell people I love my dogs because they never stole my car and they don't owe me any money.) After Trevor was arrested and busted with a stash of heroin, the drug dealers who had lost money on that deal showed up at the house and they could care less that Trevor had been busted. They wanted the money or the drugs no matter the circumstances. Jason had, regrettably, engaged these creeps at his open front door and was getting nowhere fast. To his horror, one burly thug with a thick accent swept up one of the dogs, and after demanding the money, which Jason didn't have, snapped the little dog's neck like he was breaking bread, killing this tiny dog immediately and reducing their pet population from three dogs to the two I met here today. This world of drugs and addiction is vicious, and Jason and Theresa live in fear inside their own home, lock up their wallets and other valuables inside the house, and no longer open the door to any of Trevor's friends.

They take precautions that you wouldn't expect people in a free society to need to take but they have evolved into understanding that their child's actions put their life in constant danger from people who do not fear the law. They go to great lengths to protect their valuables from Trevor as well. I asked Theresa, "Is your car in your garage?" and she said, "Yes." I said, "Did you lock the doors also?" Theresa said, "I sure did." So this shows you how they live, on guard constantly. Theresa's own daughter from a previous marriage is now a mother herself and she will not visit this home with her infant, and Theresa, now a grandmother, won't allow it out of fear that some thug might show while her granddaughter visits. What was once the dream home for this couple is now a place they live in constant fear and hope that as their son's addiction gets in control so will they regain a normal life some day.

They live in their castle that they have essentially built a moat around to protect themselves from the "friends" their son has brought to their home or other associates who know where Trevor lives. Their son, much like mine, sold drugs to feed his escalating habit, and with a $300 per day heroin habit (a mere $9,000 a month), Trevor had to sell a lot of heroin. When you must sell to feed that level of addiction, you take risks, and when you take risks you deal with the unscrupulous underbelly of the addicted. Your "friend" one day holds a gun to your head the next, robs you when you aren't aware, sets you up with the police when they get busted to save their ass and will leave you to die when you start to overdose for the same reason. They will also threaten your family when you don't pay your tab or consume what you were to sell. The addicts themselves will set up their own parents to be threatened in order to get themselves more drugs.

Jason has heard the plea that, "If you don't give my drug dealer $1,000 he is going to kill me!" which is as can be seen above, certainly a possibility. The more likely scenario, however, is that the addict needs a fix and is running out of options to satisfy the demon of addiction.

I ask Theresa and Jason what their life is like right now. They agree that things have actually gotten better than they used to be, which surprises me but let's take a closer look at their perspective. One, they didn't just wake up one morning to this scenario, they evolved into it so they have begun to accept this as their life. Two, Trevor is "in the system," as they say, and now he must answer to the law and all the strings attached to his arrest and conviction. Trevor's new probation requires him to complete ninety AA and/or NA meetings in ninety days. For those of you who don't know, AA and NA will sign off on an attendance sheet for this requirement. In seven days, Trevor had missed the last two days' meetings, but he could make it up by going to more than one meeting in a day. So Trevor is digging his own hole that he will be responsible for, and as neither Theresa nor Jason can attend these meetings for him, this stipulation is almost enabler proof.

They reason they are in a better place because they don't need to threaten or lecture Trevor anymore, as it is out of their control. He has his own fate in his own hands, and he cannot be saved by anyone but himself. If Trevor fails to meet the terms of this probation, he is subject to six to twelve months in prison, real adult prison, and I honestly think this would be the second best place for him (the first best place being a long term inpatient drug rehab) because he has to hit his bottom. At minimum, his parents will know where he is, and perhaps they can find normality while he is away. At best, Trevor might discover there is a beautiful world for him to enjoy, and realize that his parents are people who love him and who are deeply affected by his addiction.

Until then, fill the moat, pull up the drawbridge, and hunker down.

Mistake #7: Failing to seek outside help

You might be inclined to believe that you can handle this; you don't need professional help. Talk to any parent of a drug addict if you are not already one, and they will tell you they believed the same thing! I thought I could detox my son at home, and he'd be cured. I was very wrong. Seek professional help from someone who does not know your child, ASAP!

Addiction needs immediate, acute care, and also long-term chronic care, handled by experts who have been trained in this field, many of whom are recovering addicts themselves. This experience makes them BS-proof and that's the opposite of you.

90

If your children are young and you don't want to be one of the people I talk to whose child is in juvenile hall, in prison, a prostitute, an addict lost somewhere on the streets or dead, then you will stop the madness, take off your parental blinders, and call a spade a spade. Find out the truth the only way you can, and seek professional help as soon as possible because addiction doesn't get better without professional help. No disease does.

When the email subject line reads: *How do we save my son?* And the content says: I *don't know how to help him...he says he does not want to be sober, no rehab...he called me last night from jail...Can we help him??? HOW????? he is on heroin, started with oxy. Help me...* it breaks my heart. It makes me angry too. Once again, I can only say for certain what not to do. I can also guarantee you that many signs and symptoms of this son's addiction were ignored long before this email was sent.

When I spoke to parents of addicts from early teenage years to older than me, I found so many commonalities that I could anticipate the addict's symptoms and anticipate the parents enabling actions. The enabling took on many forms from filling up their gas tank to paying their drug dealers, sometimes unsuspectingly buying additional drugs for their own deceiving children. I think I took the enablers prize by going undercover for my addict!

"Paul and James"

A father from the San Diego area, we'll call him "Paul," emailed me with some initial questions about addiction, as he has a son, we'll call him "James," who is addicted to heroin. This might be my longest-running communication with a parent—it has spanned over a full year—a saga that evolves into the most bizarre twisted tale, yet stories like this are not so uncommon.

Paul originally contacted me, but honestly, he didn't want to follow my advice and seek professional treatment, so he continued to throw a Band-Aid at a severed artery. I've said it before and I'll say it again, addiction doesn't get better without professional help!

So here's the tale in a nutshell: Paul's son, James, and James' girlfriend, Gail, are horribly addicted to heroin and will do and say anything to get this drug. They lie, cheat and steal to survive (very common so far). But Paul is a clear example of a parent whose "bullshit" meter is not sufficient to filter the pure obvious deceit that flows from the mouth of what was once a loving child. Parents are too close. Parents are too frightened. When the addict replaces the child, the tsunami of crap will wash over you and you will buy it because the alternative is too painful to face. Have I made this clear?

Paul remained convinced that my warnings were too dire, that they did not apply to him, that James and Gail were exempt from my horrific accusations. No one wants to believe that their child is just as likely to do the things my son did to feed a drug addiction that they cannot control. That their child will steal their jewelry, their wedding ring included, riffle through their wallet, purse, drawers and bust little sister's piggy bank. Their sick addicted child will rob a store by shoplifting or at gunpoint, they will sell their body to some grimy stranger for the sole purpose of achieving their next fix, then they will take the drugs so they don't feel the shame of their actions and that cycle will continue. The addict will risk the lives of their parents and siblings and even commit murder to feed the demon, which will not allow them to go another second without the poison it so desperately demands. A parent will refuse to believe this. But every addict who does these things has a parent who has refused to believe it. I'd put money on it. This is not an exaggeration, because I have met and talked to many "Paul's." None of us like to believe that we could be so freaking ignorant.

Paul told me that his son James had a heroin problem that he and his wife were attempting to curtail without incurring the cost of rehab. Over the course of nine months, the father had walked in on James and Gail having sex in Paul's house in a room filled with heroin smoke; James and Gail were kicked out of the house only to return because they promised they would stop using drugs; Paul's wife discovered that all of her jewelry was stolen and the kids (James and Gail) were missing for a few days; Paul discovered that James was making daily trips across the border of Mexico to Tijuana to score heroin. Paul was livid enough to send him off to a friend's home in another state to get him far away from Tijuana and the easy access to heroin; On the way to the friend's home, James told his father Paul that he had a big problem with the Mexican mob and that his girlfriend Gail owed a thug in Tijuana $100 and if he didn't pay it directly to this thug, Gail was likely to be a goner as they would hunt her down and kill her; Paul agreed to take James to the dealer in Tijuana to pay the Mexican mob thug directly so James wouldn't just score dope on his own (I'm not the only crazy stupid father); Paul met the thug in a concrete compound surrounded by addicts in various stages of "high" where he bravely paid the mobster and demanded that he never sell to his son again (yea, that will fly); On the way out of the Tijuana concrete compound, James tells daddy he has to take a poo in the porta-potty from Hell, so what's a daddy to do 'cuz when you gotta go, you gotta go; Forty minutes pass with sonny-boy James still locked in the potty that you or I would not enter with a gun to our head, the last ten minutes Paul has been banging on the door (we are still in Tijuana and several other vagrants want to use this john as well) the door opens to a bellow of heroin smoke and a stench of piss and shit and what Paul would later describe as the smell he will never forget—the smell of what his child had become, a freshly heroin-smoked-out James emerges without excuse or apology. (Perhaps you are getting that daddy wasn't paying off a girlfriend's debt, rather, he was purchasing his son's fix).

The trip to the adjoining state was aborted and home they went; the very next day, Mommy takes James and Gail to a movie (I am not shitting you here...the next day!) with a plan to stay at the book store across the street and shuttle them home so the little angels wouldn't wander off (Mommy gave them money for the movie and those oh-so expensive theater snacks); Shortly before the movie is supposed to end, Mommy gets a tingle and decides to enter the theater to peek in on the kiddos—but wait, they are gone! (insert shock here); Mommy tries both of their cell phones but no answer (after all this they are still paying for his cell phone); Mommy leaves to go home having lost her two little junkies at the movies; Mommy's phone rings a few hours later, and the kids are upset that their ride is not sitting out front of the theater as promised—after the kids realized that the movie had been over for a couple of hours, they finally admitted that they snuck out the back door of the theater, took the San Diego trolleys to the Tijuana border, popped over for a fix, got a little side-tracked after smoking the movie and popcorn money; James is hauled off to the emergency room, spending several days in the hospital; James has Hepatitis and a staph infection in multiple injection sites on his body from slamming heroin (God only knows what else he has as he has shared needles on the streets of Tijuana); Paul pays $5,000 to a quick-fix detox center which James vanishes from before the Visa charges barely clear; Paul finds out that James and Gail are holed up in a cheap motel slamming heroin; Paul sends James to a "better rehab" (turns out his girlfriend Gail was in there) another $5,000 spent overnight and he's back on the streets; James stole some blank checks from the house and managed to cash them; James and Gail spend a few days

All told, Paul estimates that they have spent or been robbed of $150,000, and rehab at a great facility might have cost them $30,000 when this all began. No guarantees there, but I can guarantee you that it couldn't have been worse than this.

on the lam with the newfound heroin money; no-mun-no-fun so back home and Paul and the wife allow them both to move in (but with really strict rules...maybe no buttered popcorn this time!); The rest of the wife's jewelry mysteriously disappears; Off to TJ for little James and his similarly afflicted and addicted girlfriend; The Mexican police arrest James on heroin possession charges; the Mexican lawyers tell Paul they can bribe the Judge for $45,000 and get the charges dropped and return James; James spends ten days with the Federalies in la cárcel while Paul pays a real attorney to work on the charges; Paul bails James out and away they go to the TJ police station in downtown Tijuana to claim James' possessions that were confiscated at the time of arrest; Paul goes inside to claim the belongings leaving his ever so thankful son in the car after ten days in prison; Paul returns to where he left James, well-whattya-know, no James, no car; James has stolen the car while daddy was getting James's belongings inside the police station; Paul has no cell phone or wallet as he had left them with his first born in the vehicle (I hope James had his seatbelt on); Paul waited an hour before he began the seven mile walk through Tijuana to the border without enough money to take the trolley. Paul snuck on the trolley and took his chances they wouldn't ask for his ticket; Paul arrived in his town train stop at 11 p.m. and walked for a hour to his actual home; Paul walked into his home, up to James's room and into a heroin smoke filled room to a naked James and Gail who were having sex and a good old time (Yes, we kinda started here); The next day Mommy has to go to Tijuana to drop off medical documentation to the courthouse because they are helping get the charges dropped using other prescriptions James has been given; Mommy goes into the courthouse in TJ, she must leave her cell phone with the security guard and when she returns there is no security guard and no phone; Before she can cancel the phone, they incur $300 in international calling charges; I get an email with the good news that they think James is getting better because he only goes to

Tijuana to get heroin three days a week instead of five (not kidding!).

This. Is. Not. Funny.

All told, Paul estimates that they have spent or been robbed of $150,000, and rehab at a great facility might have cost them $30,000 when this all began. No guarantees, but I can guarantee you that it couldn't have been worse than this.

James is still a heroin addict and I wish him the best in his recovery. He is currently taking methadone in an attempt to wean him off his addiction. I am not personally a big fan of this as it moves you from one addiction to another. However, it is a step away from heroin, and that is a step. Paul and his wife now lock up their valuables nightly including their newly purchased flatware, but only the spoons.

Parents all across our land find themselves in similar positions, having made all or some of these seven mistakes and more. Yes, it is true that addiction and all the ugliness that goes with it can happen in your family. We parents just keep hoping, when what we need is action. We need professional help to find the root cause and give the addict the tools to walk through our world.

We intentionally, perhaps instinctively for self-preservation, ignore the obvious because the alternative is a pill we cannot swallow—the thought of our babies as addicts destroys us as parents.

Once a kid is addicted, parents have to step back and stop allowing themselves to be a part of the problem. In a lot of ways, parents have to hit their bottom also.

Parents continue to excuse addictive behavior and symptoms, dismissing obvious indications that their children are veering down a dangerous path.

We feel the shadow of shame as it casts over us, as the murmurs from friends and family begin to reach us. It is unthinkable, so that is exactly what we do, we dismiss the thought, it didn't happen, not my child, la, la, la. These thoughts fit nowhere in the dreams and aspirations that filled the delivery room so many years ago, when we cut their umbilical cords and slapped them on their asses.

The pattern of enabling will continue as long as we as parents attempt to solve our dirty little secret discreetly from behind our picket fences, like we are somehow suddenly qualified to treat a disease in a bedroom of our home. That course of addiction treatment is the back ally abortion of the new millennium, and our ignorance that we as parents are able to stop the addiction of our children without any training and minimal understanding of the demon of addiction is ludicrous! Armed with only our street-level education, we quietly and discretely usher our patient into our home and hope the in-laws don't notice that something is amiss. We will just lock our child in their room, keep those nasty friends at bay (after all, it's all their friends' fault anyway) and wait until the magical moment that your addict will tell you they are all better...problem solved! You have been sold a bag of oregano, and your child has likely never stopped using during your "treatment," and now they know exactly how to fool you until it is too late to stop.

Swallowed by the Streets

Many of the calls I get are from parents who have lost their children to the streets and to an unknown fate. The addiction grew over time, and parents looked away and hoped it would just get better, or perhaps it wasn't even as bad as it sometimes seemed. They doubted themselves. They didn't want to overreact. These parents now see clearly the many signs and symptoms they once downplayed, and wished they had risked an overreaction. Again, in many of these cases these children came from prominent families, beautiful homes, the best school districts. And most of them start by experimenting with prescription drugs they found in their parents' medicine cabinet or prescribed by the doctors they trust.

Addiction often drives these young people to leave on their own accord so they can consume their drugs without questioning, but some were kicked out by parents who had to stop enabling and simply couldn't take any more abuse from the addict. Now, these parents just want to know where their child is even if they aren't coming home they just need to know they are alive. Or not alive. After that contact, the parent will want more, because of human nature, but the fact is that step one is just to hear the voice of their child one more time.

Many addicts have sold their souls so selling their body is just another way to feed their addiction that stems from a need to not feel, and that need only grows as they continue to degrade themselves.

"Mary"

The mother of a young woman I'll call "Mary" called me with just such a scenario. Her daughter was just twenty, had five siblings who were worried to death about their sister, and just two years earlier this girl was prom queen at a prominent high school. Her daughter had everything going for her with good grades, a top athlete in high school and the looks of a beauty queen, but one injury and powerful prescriptions would erase years of parenting and moral guidance in a matter of months. The demon called, and her body answered and demanded more and more to satisfy its addiction. Running away was all she could fathom so that she could feed her addiction, which had, quickly, moved to heroin after all the medicine cabinets were empty.

Her family did have some clues that their daughter was in the Los Angeles area. The family knew it because of reports back from

Mary's former friends, and they simply wanted to find her and get her professional help. I talked with this mother for hours on the phone, and I also met her in person. She knew quite a lot about her daughter's condition, and knew she had begun prostituting herself. The search was on for this prom queen swallowed by the streets.

The last time this mother contacted me, she was elated that an uncle who had been searching for her on the streets got a tip that she had returned to the apartment complex that she had been evicted from. The uncle rushed over to this apartment and was able to locate her inside a unit with a man who was pimping her out throughout the complex. The uncle had to pay the pimp several hundred dollars just to get him to leave her with him and he nabbed her and tossed her in his car. She was a skeletal semblance of herself, with arms dotted with track marks and open wounds. He offered her a couple of sleeping pills to calm her down which she grabbed. They began the drive north to her parents in Fresno who were in constant contact with the uncle via his cell phone. Her exhausted and now drugged daughter slept through the whole trip and awoke in Fresno where all the plans were in place to whisk her into a hospital and then off to waiting rehab. They received bad news at the hospital that one of her arms was completely numb and infected and they might have to amputate it.

I talked with the mother on and off throughout the entire event, and I was cautiously optimistic that the uncle could get her home in the first place. I was thrilled when he did, and I listened as her mom sobbed at the thought of her daughter losing her arm. This was where it was left—for me. I haven't heard back from them, but I understand that once the parent has their arms around an addicted child, they have their hands full. I hope Mary embraces the love her family has for her. I hope it is her time to get clean. I hope their prayers are answered and that their family gets to put their arms around their clean and sober daughter even if the daughter has but one arm to wrap around them.

I know that blessings come in many forms and I know that losing a child to death does not come with a do-over as it is over and all that is left is a grieving destroyed family. I have met the parents who push their now crippled adult children around in a wheelchair, help them put a shirt over their head, change their diaper, hold them while they learn to walk and practice with them while they attempt to regain the ability to speak. These parents tell me they are blessed to have their child survive an overdose or return from the streets they once roamed in a blind addicted ritual. This nightmarish fate that you could never before imagine feels like a blessing to so many who dodged the death of their child. They happily go home with what is left of their children who had been swallowed by the streets.

Chapter 8: What can I do?

Addiction medicine specialist Dr. Drew Pinsky says that "Care for your children has got to be a top priority. If it's not, I would reconsider your priorities."

If you really want to know what the drug is that your child might be taking or has access to, you have all the tools to research it, test for it and all the means to find professional help. The question is; do you really want to know?

Get information.

The internet is a treasure trove of information and with just a few clicks in a search engine you can detect what that pill is that you find in your child's room, or that sits in your kitchen cupboard. Any numbers or letters or even the color and description of the pill will lead you to information about it—from the intended purpose of the drug, to the way it is abused by addicts, and even to videos showing people abusing it.

Share the information with your child.

Create an atmosphere of mutual responsibility and open communication. If you are on medication for anything and your child knows it, read the disclosure that comes with the drug with them or use an internet search engine to pull that same information. Ask your child to stop you from reading, or raise their hand every time they hear something like the side effects "may cause you to stop breathing, or death." This will cause them to pay attention and get informed at the same time. Pull up the information on drugs you know are being abused, and print out the disclosure for Oxycontin for example. Underline or highlight the word "death," as it appears in almost every paragraph. Start a dialogue and ask your child to suggest some drugs he or she has heard about and look those up as well. Talk about addiction as a disease and talk openly about drug tests, not as a threat but as a helpful deterrent if your child ever feels pressure to try a drug. Read this book, and others, together. I wrote in the first chapter how profound the effect of reading my first book was on "Mr. H," and I will tell you that he has contacted me since. His son was injured in a high school football game requiring knee surgery. Because of reading *Defining Moments*, his son chose to have the surgery and endure the recovery with non-addictive alternative medications as a precaution because he had friends who abused the very same drugs the doctors were prescribing. After the surgery, he was contacted by other school friends asking him what medications he had been prescribed. You don't need to wonder why, do you? His son was just accepted to a major college to play football. Dialogue is key. We used to fret the "birds and the bees" talk, and now we must have the talk about addictive, dangerous and deadly drugs that are now conveniently located in the medicine cabinets of our homes and the homes that surround us.

We naturally trust our doctors, and for the most part we

should, but that does not mean we can't question their diagnosis and the prescriptions they write. We need to ask for non-addictive alternatives and ask if the drugs they are prescribing are abused by addicts. If they are and these drugs are necessary, we as parents should dole them out so they don't get "lost" or "stolen." We need to volunteer family history to our doctors and do so in front of our children so that creates a dialogue which is not coming solely from you as the parent. Do not exercise blind faith. Sometimes, we might need to tough it out now and then and make sure our children don't see prescription medication as the cure all and learn by example to throw a pill at every symptom or ache. Think back to what you were given when you were a kid: The strongest thing I had in my medicine cabinet was Bayer Aspirin.

I learned how to be a father when the doctors slapped my first son on the ass. I guarded him, protected him, kept him from harm and hoped to teach him to become an honorable man, and I didn't know how to stop! We spend our early years of parenting picking up our children and blowing on their ouchies, wiping the gravel off of their little knees and trying to keep them from falling again. At some point, parents need to stop protecting their children from falling; sometime our children will need to face the consequences of their own actions or they will fall harder than you ever imagined! Perhaps they will fall so hard that you will never see them again.

Not only do we not know how to stop, we develop a shield that blinds us to the reality of what our children are doing. Many parents inevitably find someone else to blame for their child's behavior, and we parents look directly past clear signs of pending disaster as we gaze away, whistle and hope for the best in our unintentional blindness.

When you look at your child as a young adult, you can't help but envision the lofty goals and aspirations you had for them on the day they were born, the excitement you felt at their first base hit or soccer goal. They were capable of doing so much with their lives!

You can't imagine that you might one day lower your bar for them so far as to just want them to be alive. Forget the dreams of fame, fortune or a respectful career and hope that your arms will wrap tightly around a healthy, happy, drug free body who understands that they are vulnerable to addiction. That's all Lisa and I desire: Brandon alive and well. That's all.

What you should do if you suspect your child is using drugs: Two things: 1) Drug Test. 2) Drug Test. Drug Tests don't lie. Drug Addicts do. Are you uncomfortable drug testing your child? Try these tactics to ease your reluctance so you don't appear like you don't trust your child. "Johnny, I know you are growing up and meeting new friends and there might be situations where someone has drugs at some gathering, event, church or school. I want you to know that I love you and I would never want you to take something to hurt you or hook you so I have this drug test (plop it on the counter at this point) so if someone tries to get you to try something and you feel pressured, you can tell them that your parent has a drug test at home." Don't be afraid to use the drug test either. Tell your child that if they were showing signs of any disease, including addiction, that it is your job and responsibility as a parent to seek treatment for them. By the way, it is! If you ignore signs of any disease and leave it untreated, you can be deemed an unfit parent and your child can be taken to Child Protective Services.

My sister-in-law told me a psychiatrist advised her to tell a child this to justify a drug test: "I don't want to accuse you of something you didn't do, so I am going to drug test you to make sure I don't." Whatever floats your boat. In my opinion, grow a pair and tell your child you are concerned, after all you have learned that prescription drug addiction is an epidemic, tell your child that you have heard of children dying and you are going to randomly (important) test them to drag them sober through these teenage years. This is dialogue about addiction. No matter the comfort level or reception, you are talking. At a rehab center, everyone is subjected to random drug testing including staff and visitors so follow that rule under your roof as long as your child is in your home. Even after they are eighteen, your rule should be that everyone is subject to drug testing when they walk through your doors. If someone won't test, they are dirty, plain and simple. Do you want bad influences and addicts out of your home and your child's life? If so, this will thin the herd.

Each addict is unique, with two major exceptions: One, they are all liars and a lie is not a sign, it is the covering up of a sign. Two, drug addicts can't pass a properly administered drug test because as I have said, "drug test don't lie, drug addicts do." So if you really, truly want to know if your child is abusing, experimenting or addicted to drugs, you are one simple step away from finding out the truth, provided, of course, that you follow testing protocol. Many parents struggle with drug testing their children, but I can tell you that I wish I had tested my child long before he was so far gone. I have met and talked to hundreds of parents who also wish they could turn back the hands of time and drug test their children.

Our Experience with Home Drug Testing

Years ago, before Brandon's first stint in rehab, we did the stupidest thing and attempted to cure his addiction at home. In the horrid days and weeks that we were attempting to put Brandon through withdrawals (again, do not try this at home) he had every excuse in the world why he couldn't pee in the drug-testing cup. I would hand him a bottle of water and tell him I would wait. He wasn't about to comply, but was more than willing to act like he was trying, occasionally looking over his shoulder at me as I impatiently waited, and giving me this shrugging look as if to say, "I'm trying, but I just can't pee." Brandon would run the faucet water as if that would induce the flow of what was obviously dirty urine. Brandon would beg for a little rest and he could pee later. Sometimes he would swear that he had just peed just before I entered the room, obviously buying himself some time and a great first line excuse. But I had usually checked on him earlier while he slept and I would close the toilet seat, which he would never do on his own, as a sign to see if it were lifted when I returned to test him. An hour or so of him snoozing away and I would enter the room and of course the seat wasn't lifted but he would swear on a stack of bibles that he had just gone moments before. I even went to the extent of dropping one square of toilet paper in the toilet (I should have written the word "busted" on it) before closing the cover as further evidence that he was lying through his teeth when the seat was lifted to discover that single square floating in the toilet water. You need to go to great lengths if you really want to know the truth. Lies don't add up and addicts get sloppy, so this is an opportunity for you to know the truth and treat the problem if they have one.

One time Brandon went down the hall after he had sworn he couldn't pee in front of me and had unbeknownst to me grabbed the testing cup and came walking into the room proudly claiming he was clean as he held the test up for Lisa and me to be in awe of his clear as a bell test results. I knew he was lying, and I told him so. It is this simple: A test that is done while I am watching the urine come from the source and into the test cup directly counts as a valid test, and Brandon knew the rules. Brandon also knew he was dirty and I knew he was dirty if he was trying this tactic but drug addicts are first class liars, they believe their lies and they justify their behavior. Brandon at one point had a device called a Wizinator which is sold at smoke shops to look like you are pissing and it has a bag filled with either synthetic urine or someone else's. I would make him show me he was really pissing and he never fully passed one of those tests. One parent told me that after their daughter passed test after test, they searched under her sink cabinets to find water bottles full of urine, obviously clean, from another source.

Also, at the time we were detoxing we used a test with six panels for different drugs tested, but Oxy was the only one we were looking at because it was all he usually tested positive for. The Oxy line was fading and Brandon's explanation was that this showed that the drug was slowly leaving his system and we believed that. It was true that the line was starting to fade, but the fact was that he was still using, just couldn't get as much Oxy smuggled into the house by a fellow druggie friend, who dropped it on the windowsill. Brandon rarely swallowed an Oxy

The morning after I did the bust for him, he was too tired to fight the test... He was top of the chart positive.

pill when he was completely addicted as that would be a waste of the super high he and other addicts could get from snorting, smoking or slamming (injecting) the Oxy. However, Brandon also knew that he was under strict supervision, living in lockdown, and had limited access to Oxy. So swallowing the pill would buy him some time, reducing the horrid effects of the withdrawals. It does take a short while, depending on the addict's drug of choice, for it to come out of their system, but I would later discover that it didn't take as long as we were being led to believe, and he was getting Oxy or other opiates dropped off in the middle of the night. He was really never clean while he was at home "getting treated," and your addict won't be either. This is precisely why a rehab center is the only place Brandon and any drug addict should be, and additionally, why it should be in a location far from home and far from his fellow drug addicts who are still on the street.

The morning after I did the bust for him, he was too tired to fight the test. By then, I had learned to wake him up because everyone needs to pee in the morning. He was top of the chart positive. Brandon would admit to me at the end of his rehab that he just couldn't take the stress of what I was doing for him that night I went undercover the second time, and he couldn't handle seeing his mother so torn up. Lisa had been a sobbing mess, and Brandon was all she had to lean on. Brandon was not accustomed to feeling anything and this was far too much drama for this addict to feel, so he slipped away, used the house phone and called in a favor, scoring Oxy to be dropped at the house under the surveillance of a sobbing emotional wreck of a mother. She knew all too well the risk I was taking at that very moment to save our son. You know, the son in the bathroom smoking Oxy under the guise of a long shower.

Brandon is now clean of opiates after his second stint in rehab, but to this day, I get a lump in my throat every time I walk to my closet to retrieve the six-panel drug test that I keep stocked. This little self-sealing cup will test for Marijuana, Oxycontin, Meth, Opiates, MDMA (ecstasy) and Cocaine all at once, and the results will be in my hands within moments. I know that once I reach in that brown box and wrap my fingers around the test kit that I am headed directly to Brandon's room and usually to wake him up so he has no time to elude me or make any excuses that he cannot urinate in the cup. I am hopeful when he wakes that he will quickly agree to get out of bed and pee for me. Brandon knows that I will be watching to assure that he is truly providing his urine and there is no substitute for watching the act itself as it is a necessity but only if you want to believe the results and know the truth. You can also use a different bathroom, like the master bathroom, because they can't hide clean pee by your toilet. The morning is the optimum time because there is little excuse for not being able to provide a sample. Drug addicts have so many ways to fool you and if you are gullible enough (or you really don't want to face the truth) you will be easily fooled in more ways than you can count.

Brandon is now accustomed to testing, as it has been a common occurrence in his life for the last several years.

These days, Brandon knows that we are nobody's fool. When he was living at home for those eighteen months after his second stint in rehab, before he got himself back on his feet and moved out on his own (which he did just before his twenty-seventh birthday), he knew that he was subject to testing without notice, which is the only way to test a drug addict. Warning "we are going to drug test you when you get home" will only enable them to stop at the local smoke shop to purchase a concoction that will clean their urine, or purchase synthetic urine, or if they are broke and they know a clean friend they will have time to drop by and beg this friend to pee in a jar, a water bottle, or a zip-style baggie, so that they can empty the contents into your drug test. Yeah, you don't have a drug problem but you are hiding a bag of someone else's urine in your pants? Give me a break. You must not trust the addict in your life if you want to help them, and to truly help them you must seek professional help. As far as trust goes, they need to earn it.

I tested Brandon one Saturday morning just before he moved out on his own in the fashion I described above. The lump in my throat was present and accounted for as he wobbled his sleepy body towards the bathroom door I stood next to. Brandon is still 6'2" and is now 190 pounds—sixty pounds heavier than when his skeletal body entered rehab a little over four years ago. Now he is addicted to working out at the gym usually seven nights a week. He is proud to walk in the room without a shirt on or in a tank top and show off his chiseled body, but that is not enough proof for this once gullible father. No matter what, I know that drug tests don't lie and drug addicts do. I watched the side panel of the test cup as the urine within soaked into the strips of paper. These strips will disclose if he is clean from every drug on that panel. The moisture line slowly creeps up hopefully reveling the second of two dark lines which will indicate a clean test result. Only one dark line and it means he is dirty. It all only takes about a minute but it seems like so much longer. I have to remind myself to breathe as I await the verdict. Two lines form for each panel, representing each drug all negative and I exhale in relief. Brandon tested completely clean and now I can rejoice in his sobriety, another step closer to the trust he lost so many years before. He maneuvers his sleepy body back to the bed as he smiles with confidence because he was the only person who truly knew what the test result was going to be when I first woke him, and I am now the second. I prayed for a clean test, Brandon knew. And now I know for sure because I followed the protocol. Another day clean for Brandon and I am relieved but I also know that sometime very soon, I will walk into that closet once again and reach for that drug test, lump in throat, armed with only hope and prayer while I wait to see if the result will deliver the same gratification as this particular Saturday.

Chapter 9: A ride on the road from pot to heroin—Hop aboard the Rx express

I feel very sad when I hear parental denial—those of you who tell me that my child is worse than yours, it's not that bad at your house, your child only smokes dope, your child only has a few drinks, your child only takes their medication as prescribed. I remember when I was like you and I would love to return to those days with the information I now possess.

It's (not) Just Pot

In Chapter 7, I touched on the fact that prescription drugs often bring with them a false sense of safety. Now that marijuana is being accepted in more circles as a prescription medication, this feeling is more prevalent than ever. Pot has long been called a gateway drug, and the reason behind that, as you know, is that once the door to drug use is opened, it is easier to try the next one. When you surround yourself with pot smokers, someone in the room likely has a stronger drug. This is not propaganda; it is backed up by study after study. Have you ever heard of a heroin addict who didn't try marijuana first? It's not a certain path, but pot is the way in today the same as it was thirty years ago. It's not the only way in: A prescription can do the same thing.

The drugs on the street today are quite different than anything from thirty years ago. Sure you know about marijuana (don't forget the fact that it is up to twenty times stronger that the stuff you smoked), but how do you feel about heroin? I am not alone in an effort to help others understand why our children are becoming addicted to heroin. It is a drug many of us envision being consumed by the lowest class of life, yet heroin finds its way into our home, wherever we live. The reality and the crazy part is, our children turn to heroin to satisfy a craving that started from a prescription painkiller, perhaps prescribed by the doctor who brought them into this world.

You're thinking—not MY child! Heroin is for the lowly gutter slumming animals that crawl through some abandoned building, sit atop some discarded old mattress and huddle around a makeshift fire or candlelight, but not your little Johnny! Think again.

If your child becomes attracted to or hooked on prescription drug medications, he or she is hooked on the same chemical compound, and he or she will find the same physiological response with heroin. The unthinkable drug that you never, ever, imagined your baby using is exactly where they turn when the medicine cabinet runs dry of the opiates their body craves. When their habit exceeds their budget and they are so deeply addicted that their body will shut down without an opiate, any opiate will do, and heroin is the cheapest opiate on the street (also the most unpredictable as to potency). They will go there.

An opiate, often called an opioid, is a drug that is derived from the opium plant. Some drugs use a synthetic man-made version of opium but it replicates the effect. Heroin doesn't have to be slammed (injected) and it is just as easy to take today as any pharmaceutical grade opiate. In the drug underworld, the stigma of heroin use is gone.

An addict's drug of choice might be Oxy for instance, but that doesn't mean he won't "dumpster dive." Dumpster diving is a term used by drug addicts and drug abusers for consuming any drug just to get by when you can't find your drug of choice, and also a term used for highly self-destructive addicts spinning out of control who will take anything and everything they can get their hands on. The parents I have talked to whose children have committed suicide often tell me their child didn't have a drug of choice. So when I hear a parent tell me that little Johnny will take any and every drug he can get his paws on, I am very concerned. Either they just can't see tomorrow or they can't get the drugs to numb them enough to chase away the demons so life becomes a hopeless chase for a feeling that doesn't exist in their tattered minds. If they want to end their lives, they will. They don't think about the effect their decision will have on all the people who love them. People who die by suicide don't want to end their lives, they want to end their pain.

Ironically, drug addiction begins as someone taking drugs to feel something, and then they continue the drugs to feel their new version of normal because coming down means crashing (withdrawals), so inevitably an addict uses in order to feel nothing.

Most teenagers I talk to seem to have no idea that addiction and withdrawals could happen to them. They are seemingly ignorant that this is a possible outcome to prescription drug use and/or abuse even though they raise their hands en-masse when I ask the question, "Do you know anyone who has been to rehab?" Not only do we know that a parent is convinced that it will not be their child, a child is simultaneously convinced that addiction will never happen to them, even if they experiment with drugs. They are invincible, just like the parent was when they were fifteen. This is a deadly combination of denial.

I do realize that prescription drugs have a purpose and they are necessary to treat certain conditions. It just so happens that my wife was in a car accident several years ago, rear-ended at 60 mph while she was at a dead stop by a young woman who was high on prescribed pain killers (ironic, isn't it?). As a result of this accident, she's had several back surgeries. People do need medications for all sorts of injuries and illnesses and I know firsthand their necessity.

Maybe the attraction to opiate-based drugs starts with a doctor's prescription, just like it did with my son, and the drug calls to them and they answer. It always starts with the belief, "It isn't a problem, I just like the feeling, and I can control it."

But as they continue to rely on the drug, the sight of that near empty pill bottle causes anxiety and they need to assure themselves that more will be available. Other things in the child's life that once mattered start to move down the list. Family becomes an obstacle in the way of the goal of another fix. Perhaps the home medicine cabinet has been harvested for all it can yield and now they look to visit a neighbor, a friend, a relative: "Grandpa and Grandma, they will have prescriptions!"

Lifelong friends who won't "go there" are replaced by new friends who share the same goal of scoring their next fix. The new friends also spread their wisdom of which drugs will satisfy their urge, which drugs can be altered and consumed in unintended ways which can feed your desire for spending less money and achieving a higher high. Talking to a high school dropout addict is like talking to a college-educated chemist as far as their knowledge of opiates. They pass the knowledge around in an odd street level education that quickly surpasses the gatekeepers they evade.

A step up the ladder of opiates will do the trick and it will also put them one step closer to heroin. A Vicodin may lead to a Norco which may lead to an Oxycontin, or Oxycodone or Roxicodone or Opana or whatever an abuser can get his or her hands on. The drug companies' profits soar when the drug they manufacture is consumed by addicts! Does the almighty dollar win over ethics in the battle every time? The names and the formulas may change slightly because big pharmaceutical interests were not born last night. They enjoy the big bonus checks and the junkets to Hawaii for the doctors they court to peddle their companies' newest highly addictive miracle drug. Aloha motherfuckers!

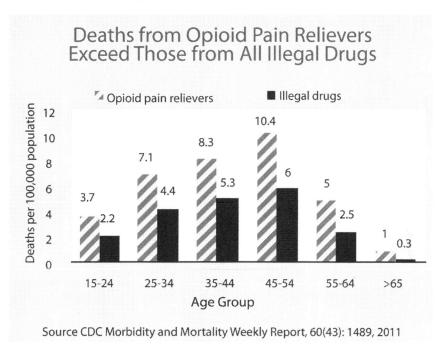

Source CDC Morbidity and Mortality Weekly Report, 60(43): 1489, 2011

Table 1

Pharmaceutical companies not only inflate the need for these medications and use heavy-handed tactics to get doctors on board, they have a history of misinformation and deceit. They are the ultimate drug pushers, and they operate with near immunity. How can it be coincidence that at almost the same time Purdue responded to the hew and cry resulting from the Fed's public declaration of the Rx drug abuse epidemic and reformulated its Oxycontin so it was difficult to smoke, snort and inject, Opana is introduced which is Oxy-morphine and can be smoked, snorted and injected and it is even more powerful than Oxy! These companies have balls the size of a planet and our government does nothing but fine them, keep the money and allow them to continue to addict and kill our children while we parents pay the cost of treatment and burial which is not covered by our insurance. Whatever that drug is now or will be in the future will be dissected by the addicts who will alter it, increase its effect and extract the desired high to feed their addiction, and Big Pharm knows it! They may scrape off the coating, chop it up and snort it, slide it around on a square of foil and inhale its potent fumes, dissolve it in the spoon from your drawer and shoot it into their veins, but rest assured they will harvest the tiniest of pills to get the biggest bang for their buck as they feed the demon of addiction.

We watch in horror as prescription drug addiction and death by overdose or misuse surpasses every comparable milestone and the deaths of our children mount and pass that of auto accidents. All from a "legal" prescription drug that is easily available to the addicts who now crave them more than they or you ever conceived. Why isn't it a conflict of interest that the doctors in the FDA have a financial interest in the companies whose drugs the approve?

My son once said in a newspaper interview, "If they change Oxy or take the opiate drugs completely off the market, I would highly recommend buying stock in heroin."

The opiate took them to a place they never intended. The child who would once never comprehend doing this does it nightly. Drawn like a moth to a flame with a similar result.

And as I have said, the ironic thing about experimentation is that a drug originally taken to feel something is now taken to feel nothing.

Maybe they never live to see a second dose—heroin is less predictable than prescription drugs, and a night of "innocent partying" can go wrong fast. A loud knock on the door the next morning, and a parent opens to the sight of a police officer and a chaplain. The parent crumbles on the porch as the unimaginable nightmare unfolds in the doorway. The police I have talked with are wary of drawing this assignment. They know that on the other side of this front door is a family who will be forever changed. Sometimes this is the same door of the "not my child" family they attempted to warn just weeks before.

I have met these parents, sometimes it is just one pill, one night and a deadly combination that whisks their child to a sudden death, taken forever and forever scarring the lives of those who knew, loved and bore them.

Sometimes it started with a broken leg and a prescription but no matter how it began, the focus here is how it ended. A future defined by loss.

Chapter 10: Hitting bottom, aka the moment of epiphany

I met a guy at a hotel happy hour in Chico while I was traveling for business. He'd been to rehab eight times. Eight times, for oxy and heroin addiction. He said there is nonstop temptation everywhere, and believes that it wasn't anything particular that happened in rehab that final time that has kept him clean of drugs for seven years, rather, it is the fact that he just got tired of living that life. The life of an addict, constantly on the hunt for the next fix and how to pay for it, who to con, what to steal, where to score, is a never-ending search for misery. It did take him being clean long enough to have this revelation but he had it, and he decided that he was done with addiction and all the baggage that came with it.

Hitting bottom looks different for everyone. There is a reason I didn't write about what was happening to Brandon before he went to rehab the first time—it's because I never really knew. Being arrested and facing jail wasn't bottom for him. Seeing his dad literally put his life at risk for him wasn't the bottom. Shooting heroin in the alleys of Tijuana, alienated from his family...it took a lot for him to realize he needed and wanted to get out.

Sometimes addicts are surrounded by their "friends" who scatter like cockroaches when one in their midst begins to convulse during an overdose. As their eyes roll back in their head, those so-called friends and fellow party goers bolt toward the nearest exit. The act of self-preservation sometimes ends with a child who might have been saved if not for their own vomit which suffocates them as they lie helpless on the floor. The simple act of rolling the convulsing person to their side might have saved them, but the others saved their own asses while another choked to death. The one who ran to safety now has guilt they will carry. The crazy thing is that this survivor guilt is just as likely to draw them deeper in to drug abuse and addiction as it is to be the bottom. They must numb the reality of what happened: Perhaps they gave or sold the drug to that guy and they must now look into the eyes of a grieving brother, sister, mother, father, as the casket is lowered into a dark hole in the ground. They are more likely to use more drugs at an overdoser's funeral than they usually use. I know a woman whose daughter's OD funeral was interrupted by her best friend's OD convulsions! If this is not the bottom, where the fuck is it?

I have read convincing arguments that say a better term for it might be having a moment of epiphany. Because the bottom can keep dropping farther and farther—look at Stacy, the child prostitute. Like the guy I met in Chico, the right time has to arrive.

Sometimes, prison can be the bottom. Although, not always, for treatment for drug addicts is almost if not entirely absent from detention systems. And I have heard stories about the marijuana and heroin smoke that creeps through the bars of certain cellblocks.

"Kevin"

In my ongoing search for knowledge and understanding of how addiction takes complete control over lives, I arranged through a family I met to meet and interview their twenty-seven year old son who has spent his entire adult life behind the cold stone walls and iron bars of one of the most notorious well known prisons in the United States: Folsom State Prison. Johnny Cash made the prison a household word when he performed his song "Folsom Prison Blues" behind these walls in January 1968, making the prison legendary.

Knowing and meeting this upper-class family who lived in a posh suburb made the thought of visiting their son, Kevin, all the more intriguing, the pending visit also weighed heavy on my mind as I couldn't help but think that this could be my twenty-seven year old son, had I not done what I had done for him just a few years before. My nights before the interview were filled with vivid dreams, more accurately nightmares that pounded in my head, because if I knew one thing for sure is that uncertainty accompanied every personal interview I had done for this book and my expecting to be shocked by the unknown was the only certainty.

Kevin's crime: Felony armed robbery and discharging a firearm during a felony robbery. He was an eighteen-year old addict strung out and desperate for a fix when he perpetrated the crime.

My interview was originally to take place in January 2012, after my background check had been completed, but a stabbing caused a lockdown, and all visitations were indefinitely canceled. I had sent Kevin my book *Defining Moments* to give him a little light reading and a peek into my soul, so he would have a better feel for who I was and where I was coming from. Perhaps he would be more likely to open up to me as he would know I was imperfect and I would not judge him.

The word came in from Kevin's mother in April that I was all set for an interview, which was set up as a visitation or I would still be waiting for approval. Kevin's mother sent me an email with the following attachment as to the rules surrounding my visitation:

What NOT to wear:

Blue denim, blue, forest green, olive green, solid

beige shirts, plain white T-shirts, camouflage, leggings, underwire bra, shoes without backs or straps around heels, gray sweats, skirts or shorts two inches above knee, athletic shorts of any kind, spaghetti straps or tank tops, low cut tops, hats, leggings.

You MAY bring in the following in a clear purse or Ziploc bag:

Driver's license is required and birth certificates are required for anyone under 18

One key (either to car or locker)

Single dollar bills, dollar coins and/or quarters (for vending machines) $50.00 max. There is a machine that will change your 5's, 10's and 20's into dollar coins in the visitor room - you cannot bring anything larger than $1 coin into visiting.

Check In:

Sat & Sun: Visiting is from 7:30-1:30 p.m.

Park and go to visitor building and wait at the door until guard comes out - this happens at the half hour mark. They will ask if anyone is going to "Camp"—that's you! They will give you a form and sometimes a number. Occasionally, the door will be open if you come later in the morning.

Go in and fill out your form. You will need Kevin's CDC number which is #####.

If you didn't get a number, go to the check-in window on the far right. If there are other people going to Camp too just get in line behind them (they will be lining up at this same window). If you were given a number wait until they call "Camp #1, Camp #2, etc." and then check in at the same window. You will just need your driver's license and the form you filled out.

While you are waiting, get change and buy a photo

ducat so you can get your picture taken with Kevin. There is a machine to your left when you walk in. It takes eight quarters. Put the ducat in your clear baggie/purse. Tell Kevin when you see him that you have a photo ducat.

Listen for "JOHNSTON FOR CAMP" to be called. This will be near the back door. There will be a table by the guard—put your shoes, bag with money, driver's license and jacket there and take your jewelry off. Proceed through the metal detector. Once you are cleared sit in the seats against the wall.

After everyone is checked in for Camp they will have you go out the back door and get into a van.

When you get out just wait either inside or out for Kevin. Since he is now at worksite it takes a few more minutes for him as he has to get driven to the visiting location. While you are waiting, find a good place to sit (outside is always his preference if the weather is halfway decent so dress appropriately).

Give him a big hug and have a great visit!

Well, I was shocked at the amount of clothing restrictions and the fact that I would need to print this attachment as a cheat sheet to bring with me to the visit because I couldn't remember all of this and one slight misstep might preclude me from completing this very important interview.

The day before my interview it rained inches and although the forecast for the next day was completely clear, it was hard to imagine, as buckets of rain poured from the sky. I set my alarm early and woke well before it went off. The anticipation and the uncertainty were not about to allow me a good night's sleep. As I lay awake cuddled up with three fluffy pillows and my Chihuahua demanding I scratch his little belly, I wondered what Kevin's cell looked like, how many pillows he went without and who his cellmate was. I wondered what his life was like and would be like until his release. I felt so blessed as I looked over at my wife sleeping soundly and I felt guilt that my son was probably sleeping just like me and not at all like Kevin.

I brewed the coffee and I readied myself to comply with the strict guidelines. All I could think of to wear that didn't violate any of the restrictions was a suit or a set of black and white striped Puma sweats which my wife had bought me for my birthday. I went with the sweats, as it would be a long day in an unknown environment. I recalled a financial planning client of mine whose son was in jail telling me that she had a drawer specifically for her "prison clothes," and she attempted to describe to me the strictness of what visitors were allowed to wear. I never really understood until I received the attachment from Kevin's mother. I assumed that she and her family had a similar drawer in their beautiful home filled with a set of clothes that complied with the rules.

I had two twenties and a ten dollar bill along with my driver's license and my cheat sheet all inside of my little Ziploc sandwich baggie. I was physically ready to find out if I was mentally ready for my visit.

As I pulled into the prison, I passed the parking area and yelled out the window at a guard by the door of this little building asking him where to park. He told me to turn around and park behind the building and confirmed I was in the right place. It was just before 7:30 a.m. and a line of men, women and children were filing into the visiting center check in building.

I flipped a U-turn and parked the car making sure to stuff my cell phone and other personal belongings out of sight. I grabbed my baggie and after locking my car door five times, I walked towards the entrance. As I approached I didn't notice the officer/guard, and there were only a couple of people at the door. I had missed the first 7:30 opening, and now the doors were locked. I looked at my cheat sheet and I realized I was in for about a twenty-nine-minute wait until that door opened again. As I stood there, more and more visitors began to collect outside the door. They were mostly women with children and a few older couples. I was one of two single male visitors waiting out of forty plus people. I began to people-watch, as this was one interesting yet silent crowd. Nobody spoke a word to each other and nobody made eye contact.

A lady with two boys about five and eight years old in tow approached the crowd. She looked friendly, and I couldn't stand the silence. The boys were immaculately groomed, which stood out in this crowd. Their hair was freshly shaved on the sides and a bit longer on top. I said, "Did your boys just get a new hair cut?" She looked a bit stunned that I talked to her.

She replied, "Yes, my sister cut it for them yesterday for the visit."

The younger boy offered up quietly, "We are here to see Daddy," as he glanced at his mom hoping he hadn't said too much. It was the week before Easter, and as I began to chat with this lady she shared that this was their Easter visit a week early and that she lived about five hours away. I asked her if she stayed at a local hotel the night before, to which she meagerly replied, "No, no, we can't afford that. I drove most of the night while they slept."

Just about then, another mother approached with two identical twin boys who looked about sixteen or seventeen. The boys hung their heads in apparent shame and stood next to an older couple just out of reach from their mom. They looked angry, and they looked like they wanted to be anywhere but here. One of the twins began to hack and clear his throat and leaned forward and spit the contents from his mouth inches in front of the older woman he was closest to. She did not even wince. It appeared almost territorial—it was so disrespectful, and it made me wonder if their lives were being defined by the lack of a father figure (likely the father who was behind these walls).

Everyone carried see-through purses or clear plastic pouches, and I had my sandwich bag, so I stood out like the obvious novice that I was.

Another couple in their fifties stood on the street about thirty yards from the front door. I wondered why they stood so far away, but since I had plenty to look at around me, I only gazed in their direction a couple of times watching to see if they inched closer as the half hour mark approached and the next batch of visitors could enter. A van came out of the prison gates and pulled up across the street from the entrance about where I was when I flipped my U turn. A guard got out of the driver's door and walked around the front of the van. The woman who stood away from us with what appeared to be her husband began to slowly walk to the center of the street. The guard swung the door of the van open to reveal a young male shackled in waist cuffs which were strapped to a belt around his body. The guard unlocked the cuffs and I noticed every single person who was waiting to get in was watching with me. Once un-cuffed, the young man began to walk to the woman, who I assume was his mother, who wrapped her arms around him in the center of the road. The father inched closer documenting the event with a small camera. I was witnessing a prisoner release and the reuniting of a family. It felt too intimate for me to watch, but I did, as did all of us there waiting. The previously dead silent crowd waiting to get in to visit began to chatter, smile and talk, some applauded lightly. The father directed the son and mother to pose together as he snapped a couple more pictures and we could hear the son say these words: "Let's just go." Off they walked towards the parking lot clutched together, leaving me to wonder how long this family had waited for this moment. As I looked around the crowd I could see a little glimmer in the eyes of those who had been waiting like zombies just moments before. I could imagine I saw hope for the day in their future when they would stand on that street taking their loved one home.

The door swung open as a guard from the inside shouted out a command for us to enter. I wandered in with the crowd, all of whom knew exactly what they were doing, except me—I was reviewing my cheat sheet. After filling out some forms and waiting to be checked in, I walked over to the change machine which clearly said it will turn my bills into dollar coins or quarters. I had two twenties and a ten so I must change these bills into coins to comply. I placed a twenty-dollar bill in the machine and chose the dollar coin option. Jackpot! Quarters started pouring into the catch bin below and I asked a man next to me why I was getting quarters. He said that sometimes the machines are out of dollar coins so it will dispense quarters. He also suggested that I try the identical machine next to the one I was using because perhaps it still has dollar coins. I gathered up my handful of quarters and deposited them into my sandwich bag. I moved to the next machine and proceeded to change my next bills and yep, it was all quarters, so I'm thinking, this better be one strong Ziploc! I walked over to the machine that sells the photo ducats and pushed eight quarters into the slots and pushed the lever forward to release a small red piece of paper covered in a thin cardboard wrapper. I removed the red paper as the instructions on the wall directed and placed it in my baggie, only a mere eight quarters lighter, and walked across the room to wait for the bus that would take us behind the wall of Folsom State Prison.

I sat on a bench waiting for the bus directly across from the mother and the two young boys with the fresh haircuts. The older boy asked his mother if they could please get a photo with his dad for Easter. The mother looked at him with a stern face and without a word he and I both knew her answer and the reason behind it. I struck up a conversation with her, pointing to my fat guppy-like baggie filled with quarters. I asked her if it would be okay with her, that I'd like to give her boys eight quarters so they could have a photo. Before she could answer, because I saw a "no" coming, I said honestly it would help me out because the machine didn't have any dollar coins so I have so many quarters that I'm afraid my baggie will break. I held the baggie towards her and she said, "You don't have to do that," to which I replied that it would make me very happy if I could. She nodded towards the boys as if to say give it to them, not me.

I said, "Hey boys, could you help me out with all these quarters and take eight of them and go buy a photo ducat so you can get a picture with your dad?" They both looked at Mom and she again nodded in this silent language, which they are obviously in tune with. They were excited and grabbed the quarters, thanking me and racing across the room to the ducat machine. The mother thanked me very politely and turned her head to keep an eye on her lovely boys.

We were soon escorted through a metal detector and on to a small bus. A very short ride through the same gates that young man was just released through, and up to what appears to be a gated park, and we were released next to a building surrounded by guards. I was instructed to check in at a counter inside the small building. The inside of the building was already filled with visitors likely from the first group. The air outside was still crisp and dew covered the outdoor benches. Families of all races and sizes were scattered within the building. People were playing card games and dominos; children were sitting on the laps of their inmate fathers. A strong flashback to the day I visited my own brother over thirty years ago crept into my mind. A wall of vending machines lined the wall behind me with everything from sodas and chips to sandwiches and chicken with rice tightly covered in plastic wrap. I guess some people must get hungry and need to eat their lunch.

After I checked in, I was told that my prisoner, Kevin, would be transported over shortly and to wait anywhere I want. The people-watching continued as I could see the interaction among families whose fathers were covered in prison tats and shaved heads. Some prisoners wore dreadlocks and all gazed at me occasionally in that silent prison language as if to say, "What the fuck are you looking at?" I was careful not to make eye contact and felt as though it might be time for me to wander outside and find us a bench. Outside, a sign clearly stated the rules for touching, hugging or physical contact: They are allowed, but limited to short embraces and subject to ending the visitation if these rules are violated. All of the benches were wet so I walked back inside to request a towel or something to dry the seats with. I was told, "When your prisoner gets here, he can request paper towel to clean the area." I walked back outside to the crisp air and sunny sky. There was one other couple walking together outside under the watchful eyes of authority and me just waiting. I had only seen Kevin in pictures and the photos I had seen were prison photos taken with his family during a visit. I had sent him my book *Defining Moments* so I figured he would know what I look like since the back cover has my picture, but I honestly didn't know if he ever received the book with all the restrictions of mailing something to a prisoner.

A young man appeared and was smiling ear to ear and looking directly at me. He looked familiar, but I could tell he knew me. He walked up to me with his hand extended for a handshake and I reached out to introduce myself. I told him, "Hey before I forget, your Mom told me to give you a big hug," and I gave his rigid body a hug. I told him I tried to dry an area for us but they wouldn't allow me to, and he quickly said he'd take care of it. Kevin walked inside the building, and as I watched him, I could see my son. Kevin is just a normal looking young adult that I see with my boys all the time, except he is wearing prison garb and living every day behind the wall of Folsom State Prison. Kevin returned with a

Kevin has grown up behind these walls and his only glimpse of the outside world comes from the eyes of those who visit.

handful of paper towels walking down a few steps towards a bench, which he eagerly wiped down, first glancing back up and me asking, "Is this OK?" I nodded and said sure. Kevin dried the bench seats and top with the movements and hospitality of a waiter who is doing a quick clean-up to ready a table for waiting diners. He passed me on the way back to the room where he must return the paper towels and as he passed, this twenty-seven year old says, "I have secured that table for us." It seemed such an unusual statement for a young man, but not so unusual considering he has been in here since he was eighteen years old. Kevin is and for all intents and purposes has always been a prisoner. Kevin has grown up behind these walls and his only glimpse of the outside world comes from the eyes of those who visit.

I could sense Kevin's guard was up, as it probably is every day of his life. One wrong word, one wrong move, could prove fatal or add years to a sentence which has already spanned his adult life. Kevin was sporting a recently stitched up eyebrow courtesy of some unstable inmate who clocked him for no apparent reason. I suppose this wasn't his first or his last as he was a normal size young man but nothing compared to some of the tatted up brutes that walked around us. I began to talk to Kevin by exchanging pleasantries about our families, needing to gain his trust and get him comfortable with me, a stranger and a visitor in his notorious home. Kevin mentioned he had read my book, and suddenly his voice dropped to barely audible and for only me to hear he said, "I'm going to say something to you and I mean no offense or disrespect but I must say this in case somebody knows who you are." I nodded. Kevin's voice returned to the normal level of sound that all could hear just as we had begun our conversation and he stated: "I need to tell you that I don't condone what you did for your son and I am opposed to the concept of turning someone in to lighten a sentence." He continued, "I took full responsibility for my actions and I serve my time here because what I did was wrong, and

I deserve to be here for my crime."

Kevin looked at me as if I might be angry and I reached my hand across the table and held the back of his hand squeezing it quickly and said, "I completely understand." I knew in an instant that Kevin was protecting himself in a violent prison where the throats of snitches get slit quickly and quietly. Our conversation continued and it was all baby steps for me as we talked for well over two hours before I felt like Kevin might share comfortably. Consistently, throughout our conversation, any time Kevin said anything to do with the race of a person, the availability of drugs, the name of any drug and anything that was about other prisoners or guards his voice would instantly drop to that same barely audible tone and then effortlessly return to the normal tone when we were talking about safe topics. It was as smooth as a bird singing and the note dropping and returning. It was all just a natural evolution of himself in an effort to survive and live to see freedom one day.

Kevin said that he started smoking marijuana at 13 years old and that was his gateway to experimenting with stronger drugs and hanging out with people who could get any drug you desired.

When I tried to find out what life was like living in a prison, Kevin seemed puzzled by my questions. Sharing a room with a killer, a stainless steel toilet in the center of the room for all to see, food that any normal person would only eat if they were starving, and the regiment of prison life including body cavity searches at will and at any time had been his entire adult living experience. He didn't find any of this odd, it just was what you get in prison, and this was the only option he had (so he really had no options). He obeyed and he minded his own business to survive.

A shout from an inmate who was working for the guards startled me: "Camp check! Camp check!" Kevin leapt to his feet, giving me just time to ask, "Is everything OK?" Kevin took off towards the door of the building, "I'll explain when I return." All of the inmates quickly headed inside. In a few moments, Kevin returned, telling me that a random inmate check like that would happen and that he was required to report in with all the prisoners.

Kevin began to openly talk about why he was here and what had brought him to this prison. Kevin said that he started smoking marijuana at thirteen years old and that was his gateway to experimenting with stronger drugs and hanging out with people who could get any drug anyone desired. Somebody could always find a parent, a grandparent, or an unsuspecting neighbor's medicine cabinet filled with anything and everything you needed if you wanted to get high. Getting high had started so he could feel a sensation or alter himself to fit in with all the others he knew but eventually it escalated into a nightly search to satisfy his addiction.

Kevin told me that his life from age thirteen to eighteen when he was busted was a virtual blur. Even after he was busted he remained in a blur throughout the trial process. The way he had acted and treated his parents was disgusting to him now. Kevin expressed great remorse as he recalled a series of failures from traffic accidents, bad grades, arrest, court dates, visits with medical professionals and failed rehab attempts where he violated every rule and essentially pissed on everyone and anyone who tried to help him. His parents finally kicked him out of the house just shortly after his eighteenth birthday and he celebrated his "freedom" with a drug induced rampage that spiraled out of control filled with drugs, friends, strippers, and cheap hotel rooms just for consuming more drugs.

He was so high that he truly doesn't remember how he got from one place to the next, but he remembers visiting a friend's home where they found the gun of a parent. That gun would later be looked at, loaded and unloaded and considered for many hours. The money necessary to buy the drugs he needed was not forthcoming. He never thought he would rob someone, that he could rob someone. Kevin sat with friends outside of several liquor stores, gas stations, and convenience stores, and none of them could bring themselves to cross the line. They would pull in and wait and eventually pull away without robbing the stores as planned. Eventually the need to get high was calling to Kevin, and he knew he couldn't survive without the drugs. At one gas station, he finally was desperate enough to follow through. "I'll do it," Kevin said to the others in their car, "you all stay here and wait." He grabbed the gun and a beanie to cover his face. He marched into the station and pulled the gun out demanding all of the money and terrifying the man behind the counter. "Give me your fucking money or I'll blow your brains out!" he said.

Kevin looked up at me as he told me this, with tears welling in his eyes almost pleading with me as to how sorry he was and how much he must have scared the man. "I wasn't ever going to shoot anyone, but the gun was loaded and I was scared to death. Anything could have happened, and I could have killed someone! I couldn't live with myself if I had killed someone." Kevin continued to tell me that he ran out the front door with a fist full of cash. As he got to the car, he said, he decided to fire the gun into the ground to keep the cashier from running out to get his license plate. This is where he made a huge legal mistake by discharging a firearm during a felony robbery.

The genie was out of the bottle, and it was much easier to do it again and again. Easy money. The next few robberies went in a similar fashion, until they had enough money for more drugs, booze and lap dances. He needed to consume more to erase the guilt and then more money was needed to feed the demon. The spree continued, but an addict doesn't add up all that is going on, because he or she has but one target, a singular focus—the drug. So all rational thinking is gone. Robbing several stores in a small area and then doing the same thing again in the same area twenty-four hours later is crazy. The possibility of capture never factors in when you are high and invincible. One more robbery and a few miles onto the freeway and he saw the police blockade, and then he looked in his rear view mirror to see the rest of the police force. A person is not taken down lightly when he is the prime suspect in a string of robberies that include a trigger that has been pulled.

Kevin said he essentially woke up in a prison transport van when he was getting transported from one county to the next. His lawyer would finally get this horribly addicted man-boy the best deal he could, and plea bargain to fifteen to twenty years behind bars—a bargain considering he was facing five strikes and life in prison.

Kevin has turned his life around as best as he possibly can while in prison. Kevin was an integral part of creating a study group to help inmates including himself obtain a degree. Kevin is highly religious and chooses to stay clean and sober in a prison where drugs can be found and consumed in every cellblock. The smells of marijuana and heroin smoke fill the air at night and creep through the bars as a grim reminder that even behind these walls the demon calls. "Sobriety is a choice and I don't make it my business if someone has a different choice," Kevin said, and continued, "I just want to live through this and be with my family outside of these walls one day." It wasn't hard for me to imagine this, as I had witnessed a prisoner release just hours before.

I asked Kevin, "What do you miss the most about the outside world?"

He answered quickly, "My family."

"What is your biggest regret?"

Kevin hung his head, "The stigma I cast on my family as the parents of a convict. They don't deserve that shadow. They were great parents, and I was a horrible kid."

I asked him, "What do you want to do with your life when you get out of here?"

Kevin said, "I want to help kids stay away from drugs and stay out of places like this."

Our time was over and I had been there for a full five hours. It seemed like a few minutes visiting with my son but this wasn't my son, although it could have been.

I sent the following email to his mother after my visit with the subject line reading: "Big hug successfully delivered."

"I had the pleasure of visiting with Kevin yesterday. I barely missed the 7:30 because I fell prey to that first unmarked road with the big Folsom Prison entrance. Anyway I made it through as an obvious novice with my small Ziploc bag compared to the frequent visitors with all the proper gear. Kevin and I talked like we knew each other for years and I left when they tossed me out via the last bus. What a great young man trapped in an environment which does not suit him or represent your wonderful family. Fortunately he has chosen to rise above his surroundings and I truly believe he will be an admirable member of our society soon and put this prison world far behind him. It was a beautiful day after the chill in the air gave way and I couldn't have been more impressed with him as a man. Thanks so much for helping me through the process. Know that when I asked him the question of what he missed most, Kevin answered before I finished the question, "my family!" Take care and may God protect this special young man behind these walls until he can walk free and prove to all that he made a stupid mistake while horribly addicted and that does not define his potential as a person. Your son is a great guy; one day a van will pull up from

across the visitor's center and Kevin will step out and give you the hug of a free man that you have long awaited.

Bradley DeHaven

Her reply:

Brad-

Wow. When Kevin told me how long you stayed I asked him if you knew you could leave before 1:30. He said he thought so but the time went by so fast he didn't really think to ask you if you needed to leave earlier. He said the exact same thing—he felt like he knew you as it was so easy to talk to you. He called us right after you left and sounded so happy about your visit. I cannot thank you enough for spending your day with him. It is so good for him to talk to people outside of the prison—he says it makes him feel like a human being which is something he doesn't feel very often inside those walls. We are in the midst of gathering letters of character reference and job offers and have a meeting with our lawyer next week to determine if there is any way to get him out before his release date of March 2015. Our lawyer is hopeful that he can at least get the time he spent in local County Jail back for him which would equate to approximately 6-9 months. Psychologically, anything would be helpful as the time is starting to wear on him. I will let you know the outcome of this, although I know things don't move very quickly in this regard. Brad, thank you. For your kind words and your time and especially for all that you do for our community. I pray that through stories like yours and mine we can truly make a dent in this devastating issue with our

young people. Blessings to you and your family-
Sharron

For some, being sent to prison for fifteen years is the epiphany. For many others, it is not. Hitting bottom is completely individual and cannot be predicted. A parent has no way of knowing the depths to which an addicted child will fall, and tragically, must not be there to cushion the blows.

Chapter 11: Ready for recovery—How do you find treatment?

Okay. Regardless of how we got here, we're here. Maybe this kid did drugs every weekend for two years before finding himself in this mess; maybe he started with the gateway drugs that many of his friends stayed with. If you're the family living with the addict, it just doesn't matter how it happened, only that it did. If it only happens to a small percentage of users, but your kid is one of them, for you, for him, it's 100%.

As parents, we tend to throw a Band Aid at a gaping wound because we don't see addiction for the demon it is; and again, we don't want to believe that it can possibly be as bad as all that. Our children slowly drift away from our families, into the waiting arms of the other miserable drug addicts. I have had far too many parents describe to me how their child's addiction and behavior has gotten to the point that they cannot even look at their child anymore. These caged animals are addicts and although your child is inside the body you see, they are lost enough not to care about you. They need a fix and the destruction they are doing to you is not visible to them. They need help and you must put your hurt aside with hopes of repairing it later. This addiction is about the addict now; later we can try to salvage what is left of the family.

Now, we need to keep these children alive and get them professional help as soon as possible and hopefully someday we will be blessed with wrapping our arms around our children, clean and sober of the drugs that once defined their every move. You need to do everything in your power to get them professional help, not everything in your power to help them; it is usually some form of enabling if the help is coming from the parent.

Recovery is long term. I believe treatment should be too.

Addiction is ugly in every way and thinking that twenty-five days will cure something that owns your every thought and move is ludicrous. Kumbaya family gatherings are all part of most short term treatment programs at the local facility and it's not that they are a bad thing, it's just that serious addiction needs serious attention and that means long term treatment, as long as it takes, just like any other disease. I also only know of one treatment program that will take the addict back at no charge if they relapse within six months of completion, and that is Narconon.

Whatever you decide to do, throw everything you have at addiction the first time. I have talked to parents and addicts that have been through six or more short-term treatment programs and honestly they just can't afford another, but in the end they spend more than one long-term treatment program. If short-term treatment is all your insurance will pay for then use it while you look for a long-term inpatient treatment program. (See Figure 6: Qualities of a good treatment program)

Can you imagine going to a hospital for cancer treatment and all patients across the board are given a twenty-five-day treatment? I get it, treatment is expensive and there are no guarantees of success, but to be quite blunt, funerals are expensive also, and I have never been to a successful one. Unfortunately, I have been to many, and I have heard the news of far more young people who are attending the funerals of friends. In one three-month period around Christmas 2010, three of Brandon's friends died of overdoses, two were young ladies. One young lady was a guest of Brandon's at a San Diego Chargers football game just a month before. Brandon had sent us a picture of their smiling faces from the game that day. I look at her and I see a beautiful young lady whose family must be devastated and left wondering what they could have done differently so they could see that face once again.

Qualities of a good treatment program

physiological detox with trained medical supervision	Acknowledges and addresses co-occurring psychiatric conditions	one-on-one counseling
assists with locating social support and improving relationships	teaches lifestyle balance	resolves underlying emotional issues
relapse treatment	incorporates the family component	ongoing support

Figure 6

Who is Narconon?

I have received hundreds of calls from parents and loved ones who are looking for help with their addicted loved one. People who are afflicted by addiction need help. This is the reason I follow my passion to help others who have an addict among them. As you are aware, my son went through the Narconon program twice. I have heard the conspiracy theories as to Narconon being a façade for the religion of Scientology or a cult and so on. I am neither a Scientologist nor a member of the Church of Scientology. I am not associated with the Narconon organization in any formal way other than my relating our family's experience and the feedback I have received from other families who have also utilized the services of the Narconon drug rehabilitation program. Quite simply, I know that I gave my deeply addicted and troubled son to Narconon, and they gave me back the wonderful young man he is today. Brandon is not nor has he ever been a Scientologist nor was he ever encouraged to become associated with Scientology while he was in treatment or after. I personally contacted Narconon and asked them to help me better explain Narconon's association, if any, with the Church of Scientology and why this was a common objection to their treatment program. They gave me a satisfactory answer and I believe this is not an insidious recruitment arm of the church.

I honestly don't understand why it would even matter, as I know that so many of us who are afflicted by addiction would do anything to see our children clean and sober again. Better than a temporary fix, they come out of the Narconon program and others like it with skills and a clear understanding of addiction. Narconon uses a drug-free holistic treatment program which is very rare in the world of rehab. Many addicts are treated with drugs like Methodone and Suboxone to satisfy their urge for opiates. In the many calls I have received from parents, they find that their children have just switched addictions or use the so-called antidote to trade for other drugs that they still desire. I know that treating drug addiction with drugs is much more common than a non-drug rehabilitation and I am sure it works for many. I personally liked the thought of getting my son away from the mentality that there is a pill for every pain. I also take note that Big Pharma has addicted our children, made billions doing it, and has deceived the public about just how addictive these drugs are, and now they make a pill that is a purported cure. Frankly, I don't trust pharmaceutical manufacturers to do the right thing, and I liken them to big tobacco, who lied to the public for so long while they addicted and the products killed millions. What we need is education and reform that will force change and identify predators who are peddling dangerous and deadly drugs disguised as remedies.

I believe Narconon gave Brandon the tools he needed to navigate the rough waters ahead in his life. I also believe that there are other long term inpatient programs that can to do the same.

Brandon walks through this world with easy access to drugs and hopefully he will be able to remain confident to resist a substance that once owned him, and hopefully he will never return to the addiction that nearly destroyed him and everyone who loves him. I have never completely read any book written by L. Ron Hubbard, although I do find it pretty impressive that *Dianetics* is one of the bestselling books of all time.

I also know that twelve-step programs are deeply religious programs. Addicts are encouraged to believe that they are powerless to addiction and must rely on God to bring them back to a clean and sober life. The meetings are full of prayer. I find nothing wrong with that approach, as again, I know we just want our children and loved ones free from addiction and living a normal life. My true belief, based on my own experience and literally hundreds of conversations with parents who have addicted children who have gone through some type of treatment is that a parent must look for a rehab program that will keep the addict as long as it takes to get them ready for this world filled with drugs. The addict has already experienced an appetite for drugs that led them to addiction in the first place. I have talked with far too many addicts who have been treated in twenty-five or thirty day programs and they have all told me pretty much the same thing: They are counting the days until their time is up so they can do drugs again.

I don't find short-term programs much different than my ignorant attempt to put my son through withdrawals and keep him away from drugs until the drugs were out of his system and thinking that would cure him. I call these programs a "cake bake." The reason for this nickname is that I don't think you can reasonably say that every addict will be done (treated) in X-number of days in the same way you can say a cake will be done in fifty minutes.

Even the treatment centers that do keep them as long as it takes are not guaranteed success, but I have found through my many conversations that there is more depth to a longer-term treatment program than a specified period of time program.

The work Narconon did with my son was intensive: It included one-on-one therapy in an attempt to discover why he was abusing drugs, how this all started, what triggered him to desire to not feel in the first place, and what triggers him to reach for his next fix. Kids for the most part can't see past tomorrow let alone into their future. The smallest things to us could be huge problems to them. It might be something that you as a parent have no idea that they remember from a very young age or something they have never, ever told you about, yet it eats them alive inside and they just want it to go away, to forget it, to not feel it. They all became addicted by starting drugs for a reason and a great rehab program is going to dig deep to find that reason and make the addict face it by feeling it. Whatever "it" is.

A great treatment program is going to tear the addict down and rebuild them before they walk out the door into the wide wide world of drugs. The addict needs tools to cope in this world and to face the problems of the past and the problems that will occur in the future; to face their former and current friends who may or may not still be abusing drugs and have the inner knowledge to deal with this without joining in or falling back into addiction. The addict needs to be taught to handle themselves in situations where they are stressed, confronted with a ghost from the past, or sitting at a table where their previous drug of choice is dropped right in front of them. They need to have the tools to just say no! They need to separate themselves from those who still use drugs and surround themselves with friends who understand that this addict, their friend, brother, cousin or whoever, cannot just have one.

I believe old friends, people who they used to do drugs with and who are now also in remission, can be good to be around. Perhaps they have been through rehab or even prison. This may be a difficult situation to grasp, as it was for me, but some of the most constructive, positive, anti-drug conversations I have heard with Brandon were when he was with his friends who once did drugs with him. It is an odd conversation to listen in on but they reminisce about the "bad old days" when these drugs orchestrated their every move. They have healthy conversations about how great life is now that they are clean. They talk of going to NA meetings together or openly wonder how they ever lived the way they did as addicts. They talk about exercising, goals, their jobs and all the normal things that one would never tune in to if they hadn't all been horribly addicted at one time.

It is difficult for an addict who is not religious to find support groups outside of treatment. Narcotics Anonymous (NA) has been building a support group for generations that is easily accessible in almost every community. My son went to meetings at NA for a long time and all during his stay at the sober living home, but it was not ideal for him. With NA, finding the right fit with a sponsor is very important. Brandon's first sponsor turned out to be very religious and insisted Brandon pray with him and that was a deal breaker for my son. Brandon told me he felt like he was lying and going through the motions when praying. He was done lying and felt that he did have the power and training to live clean from drugs and he was in control of himself. He found other people who felt the same way at these NA meetings—people who wanted to have support after treatment but did not want to pray for it. He found himself teaming up with these people at the gym, and that has worked for him. I still think the NA meetings were an important step, as he needed to experience all aspects of sobriety and apply what he learned in ways that spoke to him. Like any other learning experience in life you always hear more than you retain. The parts you hang onto and can use are those bits you can relate to. Information, training and education is like someone pouring sand into your hands and as you walk away from this, sand begins to trickle through your fingers and you retain what you can grasp.

When you are searching for a rehab center that fits your addict and your family it is all very personal and you likely know better than anyone what your child will relate to and the goal is for them to retain as much as possible. Forcing an Atheist to go to a Twelve Step program is probably a poor fit and forcing your once highly religious child to attend a secular rehab is also probably a bad fit as you might want to rekindle their relationship with their God during rehab. You ask the questions that pertain to your addict but in all cases step back when the professional takes over, as the addict doesn't need any more mothering or fathering, they need treatment. The professionals at any treatment center will let you know when and where you are needed and helpful and on the flip side they should let you know when your actions are hurtful to treatment. So listen to them. Bringing a milkshake to someone hospitalized with pneumonia may seem like a kind gesture, but it may also kill them.

Rehab centers should also help you with the treatment of your addict after they leave the treatment center and that includes being brutally honest with you about enabling behavior. Do not fall back in the same trap that got you here. It is not all better because little Johnny received treatment. Parents just want the process to be over and everything to be rosy but that is a grave mistake. Parents don't want to send away their (twenty-five or thirty-five year old) "baby" to some unknown rehab 1000 miles away. They want to visit them every weekend and coddle them. But newsflash, that is why we are here, and it is time for your child to grow up into the adult they are. Being surrounded by like-minded people far away all working towards sobriety is what they need. They need to walk in the door of that rehab day one and be that deer in the headlights. As they are there longer, they will see the other new arrivals; they will see people completing the program and everything in-between. This is a healthy environment for an addict, but where do you fit in? Calls and support, communicating with counselors, and whatever else the professionals tell you will help and not distract from treatment.

Ask the prospective rehab center for referrals of parents and addicts who are willing to share their experience with you. Research the rehab center on the internet but don't believe everything you read. This is a competitive business, so rocks may be tossed at other centers. Also, addicts do not want to be in rehab because they don't get the drug they desire if at all. They will say and do anything to get out, including telling you they have been tied to a chair and beaten. Anything to get Mommy and Daddy to come to the rescue and anything to return to their drug. They are usually adults and they can leave rehab, but rehab center staff members should be experts at convincing them to stay long enough to lift that cloud from around their heads and hopefully show them that there is a light at the end of the tunnel.

Nobody said rehab is easy for anyone involved but at some point you need to take that leap of faith because the plain and simple fact is that your addict is not going to get better without outside help and what you have been doing for however long hasn't worked and it won't work because your addict knows exactly how to get you to come rushing to their rescue.

But even successful treatment isn't always enough. Think about the success rates of radiation or chemotherapy for cancer patients; these treatments may push the disease into remission for months, years or forever. They may also do nothing for the patient, but we must pursue professional treatment even without a guarantee. It's our best bet.

Chapter 12: The inevitability of relapse

It may be gone, but don't forget it.

The demon of addiction lurks silently and lures addicts and their family members into a false sense of security. I have continually referred to my son and others as "addicts in remission" for a reason. We parents and family members want to believe that our loved ones are "cured," and this was an unfortunate lapse of judgment that is now all in our past. It is too easy to forget the lessons we learned the hard way when our child became addicted in the first place and what lead up to that dependence on drugs. We are optimistic in their recovery, and we fall prey to the very same thing that tore our life apart before. We want and need to believe this is over, but I urge you to keep your eyes wide open, for this demon is in the shadows and can pounce on your child years into the future. When it does, it strikes with a vengeance.

I still drug test my son if he is in my home and if I get the slightest tingle that a darkness is present in him. I look deep into his eyes with love and trust, but I look for the demon as well. If I think I see the person he once was as an addict, I have no hesitation to drug test him because I know when the demon returns, he returns swiftly.

An addict who relapses for whatever reason is likely to believe that he or she can handle this demon and will convince themselves that they are too smart to return to the lifestyle they once endured. The addict in remission is also likely to make a very fatal mistake in believing that they can handle a similar level of a drug they could once tolerate. They had built a tolerance for that high level over a period of time, and now that they have been clean for a while, they may not be able to handle that amount of the drug. They've forgotten how little they started with. Unfortunately many addicts who relapse jump back in at that high level and they often pay the ultimate price.

Unfortunately, I know this from personal experience. When I was in Orlando in April 2012 for the first ever RX Drug Abuse Summit organized by Operation UNITE out of Kentucky, I was looking forward to meeting the movers and the shakers from all over this land who are fighting to curb prescription drug abuse. I was also looking forward to reuniting with many fellow activists who I had personally met in my journey including Congresswoman Mary Bono Mack. It was also an honor that Operation UNITE chose my book, *Defining Moments* to be given to all 750 participants. On the night of our arrival, Lisa and I decided to grab a quick bite and catch a good night's sleep after a long day of travel and a busy agenda of meetings starting early the next morning of speakers from all over the US including the US Attorney General, the head of the DEA and many Senators and members of Congress.

I was sound asleep when my cell phone rang—I think it was about 1:00 am Eastern Time, but in California it was only 10 pm. It was my mother on the line, and she was hysterical. My first thought was that something had happened to my brother, and as she could barely gather herself, I began to wonder if Thomas had overdosed. She was soon able to reveal that there was indeed an overdose, but it wasn't Thomas, it was my cousin, Aaron. He was in his mid-30's and as far as we all knew his drug addiction had been in remission for many years. He had struggled as a youth but had been clean for about 10 years. Aaron had become quite the exercise fanatic and at 6'2" 230 pounds he could bench press over 400 pounds. He appeared as healthy as he had ever been.

My Uncle Dan—who I wrote about in my first book—was crushed at the death of his son. Like all of us, he too had thought that Aaron had kicked the demon to the curb many years before. This overdose was sudden, tragic, and dramatic—the overdose occurred in the bathroom during his sister's child's birthday party. My uncle went to check on Aaron, who had gone into the bathroom quite some time before. When there was no response, my uncle tried to pry the door open, but something heavy wouldn't allow him to push it. Desperate and now screaming at the door he began to ram the door to break it down. The noise and commotion had the young children and his sister at the birthday party in turmoil, but Uncle Dan was focused on breaking the door down to get to his son inside. As the door began to give way, he could peek in at what was blocking the door. Aaron's lifeless body was on the floor, and the only option was to break away the top portion of the door and crawl in. The 911 call was made.

As my uncle told me this horrific story through his own tears, I kept having visions of my cousin who was seventeen years younger than me: I remember the baby shower for him before he was born and visiting my aunt and uncle at the hospital when he arrived. I remember all of the family events as he grew and I recall his dark period of drug abuse so many years before.

Once inside, Uncle Dan knew immediately that his son was dead, but he tried to revive him until the paramedics arrived and took over. The paramedic said that whatever he took, it was strong and his death was quick—within a couple of minutes.

The paramedic commented that so many prescription drugs will kill you with a single dose and many people that used to abuse drugs think they can handle anything but the drugs are so powerful now that if they have been clean for a while, these drugs will cause respiratory failure and death. The healthier the person, the less likely the drugs have somewhere to hide. My cousin was pronounced dead at the scene and the scene was a traumatic mix of family and screaming children, his sister and nephews, and a father who felt as though he had just been struck by lighting and was holding the dead body of his only son, his best friend, on the bathroom floor.

I called Uncle Dan out of respect to ask if I could share this personal story, and when he returned my call he told me where they had been. In another of the incredible coincidences I've experienced through my journey, I realized I wrote this story down on September 15, 2012, not realizing that this day would have been Aaron's thirty-sixth birthday. At the moment I was writing this, his family had stood on my cousin's favorite beach with his ashes 150 miles north of where I sat looking at the same ocean.

My uncle wanted you to know this story in hopes that it might save just one family tragedy. He wanted me to share that he believes that his son starting to drink alcohol again was what lowered his inhibitions and lead him back to tempt fate once more with opiates. He said that people tell you how horrible it is to lose a child, and you listen and think you understand their hurt but in reality you have no clue of the hell they are living until it is your child. The hardest part for my Uncle is waking up every morning because he dreams that his son is alive and healthy, and when he wakes he realizes his son is gone forever. He's gone, but not forgotten. Their lives are forever changed, leaving a dark hole where a bright light once beamed. RIP Cousin Aaron 09-15-1976 – 4-07-2012.

Brandon's Relapse

I suspect that few families become aware of relapse so dramatically as my uncle did. It is usually more insidious, but the fall is always fast and always dangerous.

Brandon had been going on eighteen months clean, and things were moving on in life as they always do. I was experiencing some issues at work, and the financial stress of this had required me to forgo many aspects of my life, including the country club I had belonged to for many years. I still had a lot of close friends who were members, and since I was once President of the club, I was well known by all. I was always invited to golf junkets and usually turned them down, but I did accept an invitation to play in an event which I had played in annually for years. My first book was away with my editor being prepped for publication. I thought this golfing event would be great R & R and a chance to reconnect with many old friends in beautiful Lake Tahoe.

In addition to the work issues, my brother had been calling me to tell me how Brandon was milking him for hours and describing his work ethic as deteriorating. I kept telling Thomas that this issue sounded like something he should talk to Brandon about, not me. I didn't feel like it was my responsibility to tell my twenty-four year old son that his job performance was inadequate for my fifty-two year old brother. After all, Brandon wasn't working for me. I had enough on my plate and I couldn't understand Thomas's persistent complaints about Brandon. I said, "Fire his ass if he is not earning his pay." I was concerned that Thomas described Brandon this way, but told myself Thomas was just being dramatic about everything, as always, and I excused it as Thomas venting with extra adjectives.

But before I left to go golfing, I called Brandon on the phone and could tell immediately that something was off. He was very distraught over the cancellation of a job he was supposed to do. He was extremely agitated, dropping the "F" bomb repeatedly with his voice raised and he seemed inconsolable about this minor event. I had to tell him to calm down. This was not the new and improved Brandon that we had lately been enjoying. He was having a really rough day, but we all do; I was too! Later that day, I talked with Thomas, who told me that he had offered Brandon some additional work to make up for the cancelled job, but Brandon hadn't shown up to earn the $20 an hour he was offering. Brandon had given Thomas numerous excuses: He needed to wait at his home for the landlord, or the cable guy, or a handyman. I saw the excuses starting to pile up. This was a huge red flag, but I didn't want to believe that with all I had been going through at work drug abuse could be happening again with Brandon.

I also received a call from a friend of Brandon's who was a working counselor at Narconon, Josh; he told me he was worried about Brandon because he had allowed a former Narconon Counselor, Michelle, who had "blown out" to move in with him. This concerned me, but honestly I wondered why Narconon thought it was their business to admonish Brandon for allowing Michelle to rent a room when she needed a place to stay. I jumped to his defense! As any enabling parent would.

But then I called Brandon and confronted him about his no-shows at work, and he said he was re-finishing a desk as a gift to Thomas's daughter, his younger cousin. He went into dramatic detail about how he was going to refinish it, like he was describing a Picasso. I have learned that when Brandon (or any addict) is on drugs, that the excuses and explanations start to take on this heroism angle and the level of drama escalates to the point of ridiculous. Like when they are three hours late because they pulled over for an auto accident and saved a family from a burning car (although the next day newspaper or evening news didn't ever seem to report these horrific events, let alone the fact that they seem unscathed). It is almost as if they truly believe their own story as they create it. They talk louder and louder to demand everyone's attention. There is no stopping the rambling as they over-sell the story in a desperate attempt to paint the picture of some delusional event. I am no stranger to these signs; this is not my first rodeo.

When I questioned Brandon about Michelle, and he said she needed someplace or she would be living homeless on the streets, so he was helping her out of human compassion...Drama alert! The more I talked to Brandon, the more I noticed some familiar disturbing traits. He was talking very fast and justifying some odd behavior with reasons that did not add up just like he did when he was using drugs. I feared that he was also lying to me and he was a first class liar when he was abusing drugs. Something suddenly seemed oddly familiar with the tone of this conversation. It suddenly sounded like the old Brandon, the addict son. I told Brandon about his uncle's complaints about his work habits and urged him to get a real job and stop working for family.

But it was clear to me within a few minutes that I was talking to the Brandon I knew much better than the son I had come to know post-rehab. The reality flooded back to me like a tsunami.

I was ill prepared to discover that I believed my son had returned to drugs, but I knew it in an instant; I shouted, "You're using drugs again!" He immediately served up the combination plate he was most familiar with: lie and deny. He could deny all he wanted but I knew in my heart that this was not the son that came out of rehab; this was the son that went into rehab!

Coincidentally, a roommate of Brandon's, Andrew, was in our neck of the woods and came by to pick up some of Brandon's tools for his handyman jobs. When Andrew arrived, I told him I suspected Brandon might be using drugs again, and although Andrew strongly doubted it, he agreed to take a drug test with him which I provided from my supply to test Brandon and report the findings to me.

I also knew Brandon was scheduled to work for Thomas again

the next day, so I called Thomas. I told him about my suspicions and I asked him if he would do me a favor and drug-test Brandon the second he saw him and call me as soon as possible afterward. Honestly, I was a bit surprised that Thomas didn't notice some of the same symptoms I had noticed in Brandon given his extensive self-described experience in drug addiction, treatment, and the fact that Thomas was seeing Brandon in the flesh, not over the phone. Thomas had worked for Narconon (per Thomas) and been through the Narconon treatment program (per Thomas). I believed that if anyone could detect that Brandon was using drugs again even without a test, Thomas could, and I was six hundred miles away. I asked Thomas if he thought Brandon was on drugs and he said, "No, I just think he's milking me for hours and not working as hard as when he started." I asked Thomas to look Brandon over and drug test him that weekend and he agreed.

I called Brandon and told him no excuses, he'd better show up to work next week or I was flying to San Diego to drug test him myself.

Drug addicts will tell you anything that comes to their minds attempting to justify their actions without thinking their statements through first. They don't realize that what they say either doesn't add up or really isn't feasible. And back was the drama that was ever so present when he was using drugs. It appeared that the old (addicted) Brandon had suddenly returned. All of this behavior used to happen right under my nose when he lived at our home, but now that I had been through the addiction ringer, I can notice these addictive behaviors from a phone call with him hundreds of miles away. The distance may have actually been the saving grace.

The test he took for Andrew came out clean which provided a moment of relief until I questioned the roommate as to how the test was administered, and some things didn't add up. First, he had warned Brandon that a test was coming later that day. This is a cardinal error because drug addicts live to deceive and hide their usage. The roommate can't be blamed; He was in a difficult position and he didn't have the necessary experience. Andrew described Brandon's behavior as odd during the drug test. He said Brandon didn't want to urinate in front of them for privacy reasons but when Andrew insisted that the bathroom door remain open, he said Brandon turned his back to him and seemed to be fumbling with something. Of course, we know Brandon had a good excuse for that! He was substituting a clean sample for his own just like any addict will if you don't administer the test in full view. You just might be a drug addict if you have someone else's pee in your pocket.

With my golf trip quickly approaching—I was not willing to cancel on twenty-three friends, I rationalized and considered how the logistics would likely limit my ability to help. I could only hope that the signs that seemed so obvious were misinterpreted by me and that perhaps Brandon was just in a bad place mentally. Once again, I was denying the obvious—a behavior that comes so naturally to a parent.

Bad Timing for Good Times

It was beautiful and sunny in last days of August 2010. All of the golfers car-pooled from the valley into the mountains in SUVs. We were staying in a group of cabins just outside of Truckee. Our tee-time had been pushed back due to a frost delay, but the day was shaping up as a perfect Lake Tahoe afternoon. As I waited with the group, we all scattered into smaller groups and we spread out across the lawn adjoining a restaurant and bar. Most of the guys were seated in an outdoor area enjoying the weather with a beverage and a snack. Some were warming up on the nearby putting green and others had taken golf carts to the driving range for a little practice.

I wandered off on a hill within view of most of our group so that I would know when it was time to tee off. I paced on grass just twenty yards away from so many golfing buddies whom I had known for so many years, with my cell phone in hand. I looked at them nervously as I awaited a call from my brother who was drug testing my son. My wife Lisa waited at home, and I had been a passenger in my golf partner's vehicle. I felt trapped in what should have been a relaxing get-a-way with buddies.

When the phone finally rang, it was Thomas, who inexplicably began the conversation by taking credit for recognizing Brandon's suspicious behavior and acting as though we had never talked about this pending drug test. "Brandon came to work today, and something just didn't seem right with him, so I told him I was going to drug test him," he said. He was obviously ignoring the fact that I had asked him to test Brandon, but I ignored him because I was more interested in the results of the drug test. Thomas said Brandon had refused to test, which is an admission of using. Drug testing rule number one: A refusal to test is a dirty test, no exceptions!

Thomas said Brandon looked horrible when he showed up, and had admitted to taking some Norco pain pills after a dental procedure, but said he "had it in control."

Yea right! Here I was, pacing back and forth waiting for our little golf event and I began to cry uncontrollably. I turned my back to the group so nobody would notice my condition. I couldn't wipe the tears away fast enough, as it seemed I had an endless stream down my face. I didn't make a noise but I cried as hard as I could ever recall in complete silence.

I talked to Thomas, I hoped beyond hope that Brandon was not that bad, and I dreaded that I would hear our group called to start the golf tournament. I was so completely destroyed even though it was exactly what I expected. I just couldn't imagine what would make Brandon risk feeling the way he felt before and after all his treatment and education and even working as a counselor at Narconon. How could Brandon do this to himself again? How could he do this to his family? I was reluctant to let any of the guys I was with know what was going on; hell, I didn't really know what was happening. I needed to talk to Brandon. I needed to talk to Lisa. I needed to talk to Bryce. I needed a cliff to jump off! I was within thirty minutes of a potential four to five hour round of golf in the hills of Lake Tahoe in a group event on the final day. My golf partner, Dave, was my teammate in this golf tournament, which quickly came to mean nothing to me. It was prohibiting me from taking action on what I had just learned: I had no car, barely had cell phone reception and no way to avoid the clock which was ticking down to a point where I would not be able to talk, only text if possible for the next five hours. A storm was brewing and I was completely handcuffed!

I called Lisa first but she was already talking to Brandon and he admitted he was using again. The girl, Michelle, who had "blown-out" of rehab was the original source, but he had also had some major dental work and received drugs there. Brandon swore he hadn't returned to Oxy...yet! No matter where Brandon got the drugs, the fact was that he consumed them, and he was still an addict; he was sick, and the demon of his disease had called him and he answered. Brandon had relapsed, and we would not know the truth until he got professional help and hopefully got clean again. If an addict admits any drug use, you might as well

Remember, if an addict admits to using one, he used ten... admitting to ten? We had a real problem on our hands again.

get out your calculator because whatever they tell you they took is a fraction of the truth. I don't blame others for Brandon's relapse, which is a classic parent mistake. The person the addict sees reflected in the mirror is one hundred percent at fault for the drugs they took.

I told Lisa to have Brandon call me immediately; amazingly, Brandon called. He was crying and said he thought he could handle the couple of Norco pain pills that Michelle gave him. But he had to know better. Brandon knew that one pill could lead to ten pills then who knows from there? Perhaps he would be back to a $1000 a day Oxy habit in no time; perhaps he would be dead like so many of his friends. Opiates were not his friend in any form or quantity. Opiates were what led him to the most powerful prescription drug on the streets!

I pressed Brandon, and asked him the same questions over and over and the answers were slightly changing with every reply. I felt like I was interrogating a crime suspect, waiting for him to trip up and expose his lies or break and admit guilt. I was still pacing on some high ground near the clubhouse of the golf course and I glanced over and noticed I had gained the attention of some of my friends. Although I don't believe anyone could see my tears, they knew something was very wrong.

Brandon finally admitted to taking ten Norco just the day before! I took one Norco after a surgery I had on my Achilles tendon and one pill was too much for me to handle and I am 6'1" 220! Remember, if an addict admits to using one, he used ten...admitting to ten? We had a real problem on our hands again. Brandon tried to convince me he was going to quit with the help of his roommates and I knew that path of bullshit all too well. Nobody untrained in drug rehabilitation is equipped to curtail, treat, stop or cure the abuse of drugs by an addict. Nobody! Our bullshit meters are nothing compared to the professionals who deal with this daily. This proposed arrangement would only enable Brandon to continue his drug abuse under the untrained noses of his unwitting roommates.

I said, "Brandon you are going back into rehab or I will never talk to you again!" I told him that I would be home the next day and that he needed to get prepared to go back to rehab because I was scared to death that this was far more serious than he was letting on. Although I truly feared one more night might be fatal, I also felt like if he thought he could bullshit his way out of another stint in rehab, I would let him for now because that bought me tomorrow. A drug addict will consume every drug they can get their hands on before they are hauled off to rehab and it is a vulnerable time for an overdose. I knew I couldn't get out of here and even if I did there was nothing I could do today and tomorrow would be a busy day of planning. A plane, a taxi, my thumb held out on the highway were all options to get home now but none of them were truly feasible, and again, what could I do today but lay the groundwork for tomorrow? My phone would be my tool to start the process and I had a lot of calls to make.

I insisted that he be the one to tell his brother. I knew this was going to be tough on Bryce because I had been that little brother. I knew Bryce needed to hear about the relapse from Brandon and I knew Brandon needed to tell Bryce personally. I knew this because it is the call I have been waiting for my whole life and to this day have never received from my brother. But I underestimated how hard Bryce would take the news, and I attribute that to my forgetting how badly it truly hurt me every time my brother had lied to me, stolen from me, deceived me and relapsed time after time.

Drug addicts don't realize how hard their abuse is on everyone else. With an addict, everything is all about them, everything! They are the squawking bird still snug in the nest and they will stay there as long as you allow it. Considering the effects their addiction has on others is nowhere in their tattered mind. It takes a little chunk out of me every time one of the addicts in my life has a relapse, or lies to me, steals from me, or puts me in a situation like when I had to console my brother's children when their Daddy was convulsing on the floor. Some of the wounds heal over but not all of them; they all leave a lasting scar, some deeper than others. After a while so many chunks are gone that you just want to stop hurting so you may distance yourself from your own blood, sometimes for years and sometimes forever.

Rope and Tie, Do or Die

I was busy making one call after another. I called the Narconon counselor, Josh, and he worked with me to find a rehab facility that had an open bed. Narconon was so full that we only found an opening in their Harleton, Texas location which was another tiny town rehab center on the outskirts of Corpus Christi, near the border of Mexico. It was going to cost me $14,000 payable Monday morning to get Brandon back into rehab. Josh told me he would try to persuade management to do it for $10,000 because our family had been so supportive of Narconon and I had personally talked to so many parents about how wonderful their program had been for my son. Rehab was wonderful for my son but his disease, which was once in remission because of their training and Brandon's commitment was now staring us in the face and Brandon needed professional help again. The $10,000 would drain me to the bottom, the economy was still bad and we were still trying to rebuild, but I knew it was worth ten times that and a funeral wasn't going to be any cheaper. The destruction of my family was not an option.

More calls, to Brandon's roommates, who were being conned by Brandon to believe that they could treat him at their home because he didn't want to go back to rehab, to Lisa, and from Thomas, who said, although he only had $18,000 to his name, he would pay the $14,000. The Great Thomas to the rescue. Unbelievable! I already mentioned the grandiose versions of how my brother paid for Brandon's first stint in rehab. I am still paying the emotional price of Thomas's assistance getting Brandon into rehab that first time. Thomas cannot mutter a sentence about Brandon that he doesn't pat himself on the back for "saving Brandon's life." I am so sick of Thomas's drama and the many years I have endured it, but ever since he got Brandon into rehab, he will not let any of us forget it. I don't need another squawking bird, as my nest is full.

I don't know what exactly Thomas is on, if anything. I honestly think he was on heavy drugs so long that the traits have become part of him. Of course, Thomas may be using drugs again. Had Brandon relapsed because of his proximity to my brother? My head was swirling with so many thoughts including the fact that I was trapped on a mountain and my son had relapsed back into drugs after I had so much newfound hope for him. I told Thomas, flat out, "I am paying the cost, final. He is my son, not yours, and this is my responsibility. End of conversation!"

I continued with the phone calls between my wife, sons and Narconon staff as the golf group watched from the scenic outdoor patio, which I would not have the opportunity to enjoy. Their faces blurred through my tears, and I tried to get a grip, to settle myself to handle all I can, as best as I can and all in a very small window of time, while I am trapped on a mountain. All of this is happening while I wait to hear my name called to fucking golf of all things. My head was so far up my ass after all this drama that I couldn't imagine how I could stop crying, let alone hit a little white ball down narrow tree lined fairways but what could I do?

I watched as foursome after foursome of our group was called and left towards the first tee knowing I was coming up soon, and watching my partner and longtime friend, Dave, as he tried not to get caught looking at me, obviously wondering what the hell was going on! These guys are here for a good time golfing, not to be a shoulder to cry on. I didn't see any gain in sharing my disaster with them. Dave knew my son was an addict, and knew me well enough to know that if I wanted to talk about it I would.

I noticed I had a missed call and a voicemail from Bryce while I was making other calls. I knew he would know by now and had likely talked to Brandon. As I was about to listen to the voicemail, Dave called to me that we were next on the tee. I yelled back at him to wait just a moment more as I needed to listen to Bryce's message. I heard an absolutely hysterical Bryce who was crying, screaming and gasping for air as he attempted to speak in between his sobbing enough to say the following: "Hi Dad, it's Bryce...I just got off the phone with Brandon's shit...because I heard from mom...I don't think we should send him to fucking rehab...I mean...he doesn't need any more crutches...he doesn't need any more fucking excuses...he doesn't need any of that shit...we don't need to spend ten grand on that fucking piece of shit...I know we all love him, but he needs to figure this shit out on his own...we have too much stress at home to deal with this shit... (Then he is crying so hard, that he is inaudible, until)...I love you Dad...but I hope you're having fun...I'll talk to you soon...bye."

I stood on this mound looking down on this remarkable golf course on this beautiful sunny day. What a terrible irony that I was somewhere so dark and ugly. I saw Dave in the parked golf cart just below me sitting in silence, occasionally glancing up. I am sure he knew whatever was going on with me was not good, and figured that if I wanted to tell him I would. I turned away from Dave, wiped the tears from my face and tried to compose myself enough to walk down the hill to the waiting cart. I said nothing, and Dave didn't ask. I think he knew that one question might be too much so we waited our turn then we teed off, and the groups behind us joked and jabbed back and forth in the friendly spirit of competition. I hadn't golfed much in the last couple of years due to our financial situation. That was one of the many casualties of our hard financial times, along with the gardener, the housekeeper, all of my employees at my business, and the list goes on. There was a time that I enjoyed golfing almost every weekend, year round, but this would be my seventh round of the year—three of them this weekend—and I just wanted it to be over and to try to find a way home before my scheduled ride the next day. I couldn't have done much anyway to change the fact that Brandon had relapsed and crushed our family once again. I had started the wheels rolling for tomorrow and I would need to use text messaging, if I could get reception in this canyon course, to do anything else for now.

I turned off my cell phone. I didn't want to touch it, as I knew nothing good was going to be on it. About halfway through the round, I turned it on to see I had fourteen missed calls and ten text messages. I pulled far enough away in the golf cart as Dave walked over to his ball in the fairway to listen to the messages and read the texts as we waited on the group in front of us to clear the green. Nobody was dead, that was my only relief. There had been a frenzy of activity; Bryce's call to Brandon must have been about word for word as the message Bryce left me because the messages from Brandon were a regurgitation of his sad and angry brother's words. Brandon was no longer willing to go to rehab and he and his roommates had a plan to get him off drugs and test him and monitor him at home. If anybody knew this was never going to work, it was me. His relatively straight-laced roommates were no match for the lies and deceit of a drug addict! I'm sure they had smoked some pot in their lives, maybe a lot of it, but they had no idea what they were getting conned into. Brandon, now completely relapsed, had it all figured out and he and his roommates would go over this solution on Sunday when I returned. I knew I'd be in for an earful of rambling ignorance!

As dusk fell over the canyon, we completed our last round and went directly out to dinner. Again, I just felt trapped in the SUV because I couldn't have a private conversation. I waited until we got to the restaurant and told our group that I would meet them inside. They all knew something was up—the emotions were silently seeping out of me. It was as if the tears were a release valve so I wouldn't explode. They were all, thankfully, being very respectful of my privacy. I felt so helpless and so worthless to my family.

I called Lisa from outside the restaurant once everyone walked inside. Lisa was starting to buy into Brandon's plan—evidence of the gullibility of the opposite sex parent, the compelling need to believe in her son, and I knew I couldn't deal with her on the phone, so we decided that we would talk the next day in person. I called Thomas, and he already knew Brandon's plan and that Lisa was considering it. I specifically told Thomas not to worry about it or talk to Lisa, as I would handle my family when I got home. Thomas had not lost his dramatic approach, and I feared he would do more harm than good. He loves to dramatize every situation, and in my opinion either takes a sick joy in making people cry by scaring them to death, or he just doesn't know he has gone too far in a place he has no business being. For instance, I would never consider calling anyone's wife and saying, "If you don't put your child in rehab, you're going to be burying them," but that is exactly what he did to Lisa minutes after I instructed him not to talk with my wife. Now she was hysterical and I was still trapped. I calmed her down by reminding her how Thomas likes to push everyone's buttons and I got Lisa calmed down enough to the point where I could go inside the restaurant where everyone was waiting for me. One more call, to my brother, before I went in: I told him to lay off, and to never tell my wife to visualize her son dead, this was not the time to give her any more anxiety than she already has. "Let me deal with my family. Is that too much to ask?"

When I walked in to sit down, the waiter was taking orders, so since I had had all of one second to look at the menu and considering the fact that I was not even sure if I was holding the menu upside down, I asked the waiter what he recommends. He did that thing I hope everyone hates, and responded that everything is good. I saw the first two items on the menu and I tried to buy myself a second so I asked, "Can you tell me the differences between the skirt steak and the rib eye?" To which he smugly replied, "One is a skirt steak and one is a rib eye," and he looked around chuckling at my companions like I am an idiot for asking a waiter such a ridiculous question. At that point, I jumped up and got about an inch from the waiter's face—I do not remember what I said nor do I know what I was going to do, but everyone at the table either verbally or physically restrained me and got me to calm down. I had erupted and I am glad that my friends stopped me because that waiter was about to be my entrée!

Well, I drank more than I should have (surprised?) but I wasn't driving, so when we returned to the cabin I poured myself into the bed and I called Lisa to tell her goodnight, to tell her I love her and we would get through this together. We were both crying.

On the way home from Tahoe the next morning, I sat in the back seat and texted the whole way down the curvy mountain roads to everyone involved, wife, brothers, counselors, sons, you name it. Brandon's texts indicated that he was dug in and not going back to rehab and his plan would work with the help of his roommates. He was as delusional as his roommates were naive. I knew he was lying to them and to me and most importantly to himself. If he admitted taking ten Norco, he probably took twenty, probably even Oxy or heroin! The lies of a drug addict only stop when their lips stop moving. Sometimes their lips only stop moving when they die. Although it

I tell parents all the time that they will only discover the extent of an addict's abuse after a successful rehab, when truth and remorse replaces lies and deceit.

was not Thomas's place to suggest to my wife that we would be burying Brandon, we all knew this stuff was lethal, and we needed to be on the same page as a family and get Brandon back to rehab where there would be no chance that he could get his hands on any opiates or whatever he was taking. Only after that would we potentially find the truth and learn just how far back Brandon had fallen. I tell parents all the time that they will only discover the extent of an addict's abuse after a successful rehab, when truth and remorse replaces lies and deceit.

I arrived at my home at about noon and had a brief talk with my wife who told me that Brandon's plan sounded feasible to her. Though we were stressing about the money to get him back in to rehab, I had already texted Josh at Narconon and asked him to find a list of flights to this remote Texas location departing today and to text me the findings. I called Brandon, who began to tell me that he and his roommates were going to handle the relapse by taking turns monitoring him and testing him daily. I told Brandon to gather up his roommates where we could talk about this plan on the speakerphone. As soon as everyone was on the phone, I asked the roommates how their first night watching Brandon went, to which they responded that it went fine. I then asked Brandon to tell me again how many Norcos he took last night. Brandon responded, "Ten or twelve. And I took the last one around midnight." To say the roommates were shocked would be an understatement. I know these young men, and I know that they are no match for the lies of a drug addict, so I asked them again, "How did your first night watching Brandon go?" and they both had a change of answer: "Not very good." I told them that I understood that they were trying to help a friend but as they could now see, they were not able to help him and it wasn't their responsibility. They needed to help Brandon by getting him on a plane ASAP.

Brandon became very aggressive and agitated on the phone.

The excuses (justification) for him not going to Narconon were coming out of his mouth as fast as he could say them. The late, great Amy Winehouse wasn't making a joke in her song; when daddy says you're going to rehab, they ALL say no-no-no! I ended my response to him with the same answer for every excuse he had.

Brandon said, "I not going to have you spending your last ten thousand dollars on me and holding it over my head for the rest of my life!"

I said, "You are going to pay me back when you get better and isn't that exactly what an addict would say to his family when you were working at Narconon to keep from going to rehab?"

Brandon: "It's a cult, and they are just going to brainwash me!" Me: "Isn't that exactly what an addict would say to his family when you were working at Narconon to keep from going to rehab?" Brandon: "I can handle this myself and I'll test every day!" Me: "Isn't that exactly what an addict would say to his family when you were working at Narconon to keep from going to rehab?" Brandon: "I'm not that bad, I can wean myself off and I'll be better!" Me: "Isn't that exactly what an addict would say to his family when you were working at Narconon to keep from going to rehab?" I was using the training Brandon shared with me against him.

While this was going on, Lisa called one of the roommates from her cell phone, so he stepped away to speak to her. He told her that they couldn't handle him and they would do whatever we said. My team to extract Brandon and get him to the professional help he needed was taking formation.

Brandon was screaming by now and completely out of control, and then Andrew told us that Brandon had run out of the room.

I said, "Go get him and drag his ass back to this phone and don't let him out of your sight." And Andrew, who is a big guy, did just that. Brandon was adamant that he was not going to go to rehab, so I told him that he was either going or as far as I was concerned, he was not a member of this family and gone to all of us! I was not bluffing because I could tell by his actions that he was in bad shape. I knew that if I could get Brandon to a rehab facility that soon the cloud would lift after he went through withdrawals, and perhaps he would be honest with us and more importantly, honest with the staff and himself because that is essential to success!

Brandon half-ass agreed and said, "Fine, I'll go. But you'll see it will be a waste of money because I don't need to go this time, and I was never ready to go the first time I went in!" He was lashing out at everything, and his lies were as transparent as a new glass stem pipe.

Yes, the money is a big deal. There is no way around it. It is a big deal for the family who can't easily afford it and for the addict who doesn't believe he is worth it. The cost of treatment is a natural objection by the addict who is dug in and doesn't want to go and the parent is either unable to come up with the money or it will stretch them so tight that it could break them financially. Everyone doesn't have thirty grand lying around in a rehab fund and that is just a fact of life. Sometimes the parent justifies their willingness to help the addict at home because they just can't part with the money. Unfortunately, they may lose more than that from stolen jewelry, missing checks cashed, a stolen ATM card, wrecked cars, and legal costs and in the end they will find the money for a funeral. I went to one home where the addicted child sold almost everything in the family's five-thousand square foot home while the parents were out of state at a family wedding. They came home thinking they were robbed until they realized that about the only thing left in the home was the addict's bed! I told you, they get sloppy. My advice: Find the money for a proper rehab.

I had since received the text from Josh showing several flight options to Texas. One flight had one stop in Houston and then flew directly to Harlingen where Narconon would have a staff member waiting to pick him up and transport him. The flight left in about two hours. Brandon, after reluctantly agreeing to return to rehab, went to his room to pack a bag, and Andrew agreed to escort him to the airport. A few tense minutes went by and every second counted, so I asked Andrew where Brandon was now and he said he had gone in the bathroom to take a shower after tossing some stuff in a backpack. I said, "Go kick down the fucking door if you have to and don't take your eyes off of him! He could have ten Norcos with him now!" One of the many things I have learned through all of this is that when a drug addict knows he's going to rehab, he or she will take every drug they have because this is the last chance for a while. A great amount of addicts die the day they are going to rehab or the day before they go to jail! They see it as their last hurrah and sometimes it is exactly that. I told Andrew to search every nook and cranny of everything he was bringing also. You could hear Brandon screaming at Andrew when he jimmied the bathroom lock and opened the door, "Get the fuck out of here!"

I could hear Andrew tell him, "Your Dad is on the phone and he told me not to leave your side!"

To which Brandon screamed back, "Fuck you! Fuck all of you!"

The flight was leaving at 3:30 and they were forty minutes from the San Diego airport so there was no time to waste. This was all going down quick and it needed to. We were multi-tasking like never before. I told Lisa to go online and she booked the flight and printed the boarding passes. I got Andrew's email at the house so we could email him the boarding passes as well as a letter authorizing Andrew to escort Brandon to the gate where Narconon had arranged to have an airport marshal put his fucked up ass on the plane. This was all happening at a lightning pace and needed to go off flawlessly, or Brandon could change his mind. Because he was twenty-five years old, he could refuse to go forward at any point, so I needed to act fast while he was willing to go, if you call this willing.

Andrew got what he needed from the emails and headed out the door towards the airport. It was a long drive for Andrew, and he had been a champ through all of this, above and beyond what any roommate/friend should have to do. I honestly think Andrew was feeling relieved that this was all he needed to do, as opposed to the elaborate plan in which he would have to be responsible for the detox and rehab of Brandon at their home. This is what a real friend does; compare this to the one that dumps you on a doorstep or in a gravel parking lot when you're OD-ing.

I snapped a picture of Brandon's dog Molly (the white Pit Bull who we inherited from him and we have grown to love) and I texted him the picture with a message that said, "Get better Daddy!! We all love you and this is the best way for you to get healthy again!!" I did this because I felt like I needed to give him something to care about that he couldn't lash out at.

At 1:55 pm Brandon texted me back: "I am going to work my ass off and get back to the real Brandon, sorry I acted like an asshole I should of just said thank you."

I replied, "You are welcome and we understand. See you soon!!"

Brandon replied "I'm not letting this happen again," then he asked me if I would tell his uncle Harry, and I told him not to worry about that, I would handle it, just as we would handle breaking the bad news to the rest of our family and a few close friends. I would also need to tell my book editor, as we no longer had a happy ending for *Defining Moments*. Brandon texted me when he got to Houston to tell me he made his connecting flight. I texted, "make your Mama proud (& me too)" to which he replied, "Will do."

A brief post on his Facebook page via his cell phone read: "I just woke up in Houston and I don't know how I got here, but now I'm off to some little town nowhere in Texas." The next call we got was hours later from the Narconon center in Harlingen, Texas, a relatively short plane hop from Houston to this tiny town which is a stone's throw away from Mexico's border. Not very comforting. By this point we were on a mental rebuilding process after the drama of the whole event. Lisa and I were emotionally exhausted and even though we knew Brandon was on his way to the rehab facility, we couldn't entirely unwind; it felt like my entire body was a knot.

Now Arriving

A man on the phone introduced himself to us as Marco, a counselor from Narconon in Harlingen, Texas. Marco wanted to let us know that Brandon had been picked up at the airport safely, obviously high as he had taken the last of his stash on the plane, as he, like so many other addicts on their way to rehab knew that once he reached his final destination of the rehab center, that these drugs would be discovered no matter how well they were hidden. This is why so many addicts overdose and die on the eve of rehab admission. This is why the time to go to rehab is now, not next week or after your birthday or whatever, it is now or you may never celebrate the next birthday. If you feel like I am repeating myself, it's because I am! It is that important that this sinks into your head, addiction does kill! Accident, overdose, prison, prostitution, disability, suicide, murder, are all included in the package of addiction.

Brandon spent the next week or so going through those oh so familiar withdrawals and after that working hard to come clean on whatever he had been withholding that caused him to return to this dark place. Narconon once again would put him through the process and hopefully he would embrace their guidance and try to discover the root causes of this relapse. Hopefully this time he would be one hundred percent honest with them during his treatment. Perhaps they would uncover some triggering event that he was unwilling or unable to disclose the first time around.

After Brandon completed the first time through the rehab program and worked there, my wife and I had bought him a small car. It's not much, and it had a salvage title, but we wanted to help him in his new start at life. He was very appreciative. One condition attached to this gift was that Brandon stay clean. I told Brandon that this car would be sold if he chose to use again. He could learn the bus schedule when he got out. I had gone above and beyond, from risking my life to being as supportive as I could be, and so had his mother and brother.

I asked Brandon's roommates to search every inch of Brandon's room and car and that Bryce and I would make a road trip to pick up the car and his belongings. Brandon's other roommate sent me a picture of what he found at the bottom of a garbage can. I am sad to say it was used stem pipes and foil covered in black lines. There are too many foils and black markings to count in this picture. The stem pipes are makeshift from plastic pen housings. In the picture, most of the pipes, which resemble a small drinking straw, are now split in half, evidence that the addict scraped them for residue in an attempt to get high again. The stickiness of the substance and the fact that he was scraping the stem pipes points directly to black tar heroin. Not Oxy but its cheaper cousin! Brandon was heading in a downward spiral at a fast pace.

I showed my wife the picture, and when she digested what this picture meant, that Brandon had been smoking opiates, either oxy, heroin or both, she looked at me and began to cry. How could it get this bad so fast? Will Brandon ever be better?

Brandon was addicted to Oxy, an opiate, and now any opiate will do, and the cheapest opiate on the streets is heroin, and the evidence is clear that he went there. Brandon has an illness, a disease, and although it had been in remission, it was now back in full force. Dashed was my optimism that my son was cured. In its place is anger over the reality that a substance aggressively peddled by its manufacturer, a legal drug that sits on the shelves of pharmacies, doled out by our misinformed or dirty doctors, sold by the greedy recipients of a legit prescription, peddled on the streets as a recreational drug and found in the medicine cabinets across America calls to Brandon and so many other addicts every day. Those addicts answer that call without regard to anyone, including themselves, as it now owns them. Disease or not, it annihilates you to watch a loved one destroy themselves and wipe out your entire family like a beachfront hut in a Tsunami. But ask an addict and they will quickly tell you that they are only hurting themselves. They can't and won't see the casualties that lie in the wake of their addiction, until they are clean.

Relapse happens. But so does recovery. The difference, of course, is that one is quick and easy and the other is hard work, sometimes every moment of every day.

Chapter 13: Brandon can feel

Brandon was now safely in rehab—again, and we were relieved. I tell parents all the time that the best night's sleep they will ever have is after the roller-coaster ride of addiction with a loved one when you finally get them in a treatment program. You just lay your head down on that pillow after all the drama and uncontrollable thoughts of impending doom. Your mind shuts down for the first time in longer than you want to remember, and your body falls in to a long-deserved sleep. Gone for that night are the sounds of sirens or the fear of a late night knock at the door. Someone else who treats addiction has your child tonight, and you can drift off to an unfamiliar state.

Brandon would begin the daunting task of withdrawals immediately and these withdrawals will only be more difficult because of his recent last hurrah! And then he would begin another journey into his soul. He's got to journey deep into his thoughts and distant dark places to discover what had been missed in his treatment the first time, what he had failed to disclose or discover, that had triggered him to abuse drugs again after over eighteen months clean. Knowing what Brandon had learned, seeing how and where he has lived, watching him blossom into the beautiful young man and person he had become made it all the more difficult for us to wrap our heads around. Why? The demolition of our family once again? Why—what—how? Much as I was trying to hold our family unit together, I felt them slipping between my fingers like a handful of sand. I felt the trickle of broken hearts and tattered minds as the pile of emotions dwarfs what remains within my control.

The news spread, and family and friends were contacted. Once again the stigma of addiction cast a dark shadow over our family. Others wonder why Brandon doesn't just stop. Why did he do this to himself again? What is wrong with Brandon? Do I distance myself from this doomed and damaged soul? Is the end of our son, their sibling, cousin, grandchild or friend in sight? The endless thoughts of what others will think are an unfortunate side effect to having an addict among you. Coping with that stigma and trying not to let it affect you is easier said than done. I know he is sick, but those who haven't had a front seat to addiction find it all too easy to criticize my family.

Those who have felt and experienced the sting of addiction firsthand are far more understanding and you can find peace and solace in that group of those afflicted by addiction. You hope and you pray to your God, you dig deep into your soul, begging that your child will one day find peace within their own body and walk this earth breathing deep and finding that a life without drugs is not only possible but wonderful. The alternative looms in your mind, and you push it aside just like you did so many of the signs of their addiction long before it got this grave.

Brandon was safely at rehab and out of withdrawals again within a week. He seemed to be in a very good place, both physically and mentally. It is as if he was sideswiped by a car and dazed but lived to tell about it. Seemingly puzzled by his quick relapse and the degree he fell so quickly, he spent a good deal of the early days trying to wrap his head around how it all happened so quickly and after all his training at Narconon as a student and even as a staff member.

People ask me all the time, "Why did he relapse?" "When will he be cured?" Normal questions, I guess, but I have come to realize that they are very ignorant questions. The answers are, "Because he is an addict," and "Never."

I will tell you that Brandon's return to rehab went better than expected. Brandon was still going to be inpatient for as long as it took to get his mind clear and for him to be completely honest with the staff about what was triggering his desire to repeat the same destructive behavior. Brandon spent over three months in treatment this second time. Narconon absolutely custom built his treatment to match his knowledge of their program and his symptoms, common for an ex-staff member who is so familiar with the program. Drug addicts are master manipulators, and Brandon was no exception. He admitted to me later that, given that he had actually worked at Narconon, he was capable of using their treatment methods and tactics to try and fool them. He went through the motions he knew they expected, and he tried everything to bullshit his way out in the beginning. They wouldn't buy it. He finally gave in and realized that if he didn't completely surrender himself to treatment, his life would never change and he finally released and came to grips with the fact that he did hate his life as an addict, and only he could choose to change it.

At last, while in treatment, he opened up and regurgitated everything real and imagined that was making him not want to feel. He didn't want to feel good, bad, cold or hot...nothing. Brandon had been drugging himself for so long that he had grown up not feeling pain, remorse or emotions about anything. It is so hard to imagine not feeling anything, but I understand that there have been many times in my life that I wish I didn't feel. Most of those moments were during the most difficult times with my son or my brother Thomas or my father or stepfather, and they were all addicts. It is sad that the addict's unwillingness to feel is an additional burden on those who love them and care for them. It is like trying to rescue a trapped animal that bites and scratches at you because it only sees you as an intruder out to hurt it, when all you want to do is help. The addict backs as far away as possible to avoid your grasp. An addict's inclination to keep you away at a time they need you most is only because they see you as something standing in the way of their feeding their addiction.

It is sad and so difficult to be rejected by your addicted loved one when you know your intentions are nothing but good and after all the hell they have put you through. It is a grim reality of addiction, but I urge you to never stop reaching because your child is trapped, helpless and needs your love and hopefully that love will guide you to professional help. It takes time to coax the addict completely out and even then they may retreat or relapse after treatment. It is possible through professional help and the love and support of a family to get your loved one back. It is also very difficult for all who have been afflicted by the addict to forgive, and it may take years or never occur for some. At some point some people have just had enough, and they realize that nothing good happens around their addict, so although they can still forgive them, it doesn't mean they want to be a part of their life.

I consider my relationships (or lack thereof) with my father Richard and older brother Thomas to be in the abyss. To me they are lost souls and destructive abusive people, they just happen to be my biological family and they are also addicts without a desire to change or just unable to after so many years of abuse. I cannot subject myself or my wife to their abuse because it is quite simply unhealthy. It may be difficult to grasp that I forgive them for their actions and at the same time I describe them. At the time they did these things to me or my family, I hated them for it and now I understand they are sick. It is possible to forgive and not communicate with someone and just because they are family doesn't require me to drop by for a visit as if nothing was amiss. If they were friends or acquaintances, I would have stopped trying long ago but you can't pick your family.

The days of treatment went slowly but I was not impatient and neither was my wife. Our hopes of our son's addiction being gone forever, cured, had been dashed, so we were more cautious than we were when he was in rehab the first time. We were wiser and had a better understanding that addiction was a disease and Brandon was in remission until he relapsed. Now Brandon was in rehab again and we gained from this experience. It is almost as if Brandon needed to relapse to check him, to humble him and cause him to understand that this was a demon who could return with the slightest of slips. Brandon couldn't handle drugs at all, and he knew that now because addiction had sucked him back with little warning. He needed to be afraid of the power of addiction and to know that he had to overpower addiction and take control of his life. Brandon needed to feel the good, bad, cold and the hot that is life. He needed a plan to live in a world where a drug can be found in every square block, no matter if you lived across the world or back in your old neighborhood. As a good friend of mine says, addiction happens on Park Avenue or a park bench. Drugs and the temptation to fall back into that lifestyle of addiction would call to him emotionally, physically, and in the form of co-workers, friends, and acquaintances, or in any infinite number of scenarios.

He finally gave in and realized that if he didn't completely surrender himself to treatment, his life would never change.

While Brandon was in rehab in Texas, Lisa and I were tasked with the responsibility of retrieving Brandon's belongings from the San Diego area. This was no short jaunt for us at about six hundred miles but we were again the ones the responsibility had fallen on. Brandon had amassed some decent furniture and a bedroom set, so since our spare bedroom was wide open, we could put his belongings in there. The stuff just couldn't be left with his old roommates as they were looking at a replacement roommate for him to help pay the rent. More importantly, the car we had given Brandon after his first rehab stint down there also needed to be retrieved. The whole project was a logistical nightmare with the plan being Lisa driving Brandon's car back while I used our SUV to tow a large U-Haul trailer through LA and its world famous traffic. Oh boy!

We planned a short stop to break up the trip at my brother Harry's home in LA, spend the night, a southbound down and back to San Diego to pack haul and retrieve Brandon's things and meet with two very agitated roommates and then spend another night in LA before we drove the remaining four hundred miles home to unpack and return the trailer. It all sounded workable as far as planning goes, but I will tell you that I am getting too old for this shit! Lisa was priceless as my lane-changing assistant—we communicated with blinkers and cell phones so she could assist me in obtaining lanes when drivers were more likely to step on the pedal and block me when I signaled to move this behemoth trailer than they were to show some common courtesy. It was a great system. Lisa could have been home two hours sooner if she had abandoned me. It was a very long three days and the final leg home took additional hours, as the fully loaded trailer was a handful. When we finally arrived in Sacramento, I could untangle my white knuckles and drag my dead ass out of the seat. Lisa wasn't much better, having just driven this little Hyundai for half a day, when she has endured nine back procedures over the last few years (as a result of that accident where she was rear-ended by the driver high on pain meds) and is accustomed to a bit more comfort.

It was more than a little difficult to make these sacrifices as I pictured our son in some therapy session or napping by the pool when his mother and I were busting our butts because he had relapsed. I knew our youngest son was so angry about his brother's relapse that he couldn't say his name without a profanity attached. The rest of our friends and family all knew, as our dirty little secret was anything but a secret—the news was spreading like a California wildfire through everybody and anybody who remotely knew our family. I felt the shame of it all even as I drove alone down the highway. I felt the pain for my child and had a lot of time to wonder if he will ever live a normal life, as the mile markers pass by all too slowly, just as his days clean and sober will. I found myself wondering why we do all that we do for our children when they might end up on a couch someday bitching about how we failed them anyway. Parenting can be a very thankless process but I try to remember all of the moments in this life that make it all worthwhile. That is a pretty tough task when your child has become deeply addicted, fighting to get and stay clean.

Brandon was inpatient for three months and was approaching his release back into the real world. There would be no family trip to his graduation ceremony this time, and I suddenly realized why we had seen so many graduates finish the program without family present at the ceremony the last time around. Brandon would graduate with his fellow students in Nowhere, Texas, alone, but not because we didn't love him, it was because we did, and we knew he needed to know he was a man, and he needed to become one on his own. We wouldn't have spent the time and money if we had cast him aside, and neither would the others students' families. I know now that there was a family behind every student in the program who loved them, believed in them and hoped and prayed for a better life for them, or they would have never been there.

The Narconon staff counseled us as parents. Dennis was particularly blunt when he described our helping and parenting as enabling, plain and simple. Dennis encouraged us to get Brandon into a sober living home and help as little as possible financially. Every penny we would give Brandon would free up the pennies in his pocket for drugs. In fact, anything we gave Brandon needed to be accounted for, written down and agreed to be paid back through future employment.

Brandon would need our help financially because he had nothing and that was a simple fact. The way we handled the financial support needed to be as a debt not a handout. That support would cease at the first sign of drug use, and he knew he was one dirty test away from losing his family. More than that, I truly think he wanted it this time, for himself. Brandon needed to rebuild his self-esteem and he would need to do that himself. To rebuild himself he would need to start from the bottom, and that would be in a sober living home surrounded by recovering addicts just like him.

Chapter 14: How do you support an addict in remission?

Before Brandon was released from treatment, the staff assisted him with the loose ends that follow an addict after treatment. This was done both times he was in rehab. Unattended items in an addict's life are like the gum on the shoe they left in their bedroom before they were hauled off to rehab. The issues don't go away, if anything they lie in wait, sometimes increasing in size. Fines, unpaid rent and utilities, health and dental work and an abundance of surprises, legal, financial and emotional. Those items just hibernate and await your addict's return. The staff at Narconon helped research any outstanding warrants, fines or fees, helped him communicate with those entities, and assisted him with creating a plan to satisfy those obligations. He would have payment arrangements with everything from courts to utilities and almost all of them were accommodating. This to me is all part of any good rehab program and should be something you discuss with any prospective center.

In order to best support an addict in remission, without falling into the trap of enabling their return to drug use, without once again becoming a victim of their lies and deceit, several things need to happen. At the direction of his counselors at Narconon, Brandon created a plan for himself and presented it to us and also to his counselors. The counselors wanted specific details and so did we. Brandon put together a note that included everything from where he would live to how he would look for a job.

A parent can support an addict in remission by 1) Expecting him/her to meet obligations: financial, domestic, treatment 2) Expecting him/her to follow rules of sober living, including random drug testing 3) Expecting him/her to obey all laws.

Regarding meeting financial obligations, this might include paying back debt owed to his parents and others incurred when he was an addict and when he was receiving treatment. Even though this may seem like a lot for a recovering addict who is basically homeless and without income to take on, I believe the addict acknowledging these debts is as important as when the addict calls to apologize to you for all the hurt they have caused. This is part of the hurt, and the addict needs to take ownership and handle this upfront so it doesn't haunt them. The addict may never be able to pay these back, or it may happen by earning it from chores or payments. The important thing here is that the addict comes clean, not just from drugs but emotionally, figuratively and financially. It's time to man-up.

Even after the ground rules are established, there are some things that can't be addressed with promises or contracts: The sibling relationship and how the siblings see the parents' handling of the addicted one, for instance. I completely understand how the sibling of an addict feels because I am one. I am that younger brother who wants to believe in his brother but has been burned so many times that the love becomes conditional unlike a parents' unconditional love. Brandon is my son and I am his father and that will never change. I do love him and I do forgive him, but he will need to earn our trust back. I know Lisa feels the same and I also know he has a long way to go with his brother. I get it, and I knew that one of the most difficult things about Brandon's return from rehab would be the dynamic with his brother. Bryce is not as forgiving or as willing to trust his brother as we are. It is family collateral damage.

When I have asked pairs of siblings—one an addict, one not— who got the most attention during their upbringing, inevitably the addict states that the other one, the "good child" was the family favorite and that he was ignored because he was the fuck-up. Think of Steven and his brother Troy. When I ask the non-addicted sibling (the "good child" as the addict refers to them) the same question they feel the addicted child got all of the attention. The non-addict child remembers everything being about the addict. This child has felt the stress personally and seen the effect on their parents and feels neglected among all the mayhem the addict causes. The non-addicted child resents the addicted child for all the mayhem, whether it is stealing, lying, tearing the parent's marriage apart, taking time for court appointments or counseling; the non-addicted child feels neglected. The addict is causing chaos and the addict can't feel anything so they don't see the damage they are doing. The addicted child is the train wreck the non-addicted family members are forced to watch. As a parent, I think how easy my non-addict was to raise, how simple it was to attend a sporting event instead of a court appearance. But I also see how much of my time I spent on the addict. I look back and feel the same way when I think of my brother. Thomas wasn't holding his sobbing mother after a visit to the penitentiary in Texas, it was me! Thomas just told us what he wanted and needed in prison while we were there and we put more money on his account even though we could barely afford to fly to Texas and rent a hotel room just to see him. Thomas didn't see or feel the pain of my mother on that trip, I did, and I felt my own pain. Thomas doesn't feel the pain of deceit when he lies and steals from me and comes back the next day for more, I do. But the addict just doesn't feel and in the end that is exactly what they seek, feeling nothing is precisely how they survive another day.

Before Brandon's return from rehab on December 11, 2010 my wife and I went on a road trip to the northern California coastal area to try to reconnect as a married couple in these trying times and get on the same page in our reception of Brandon and his homecoming. Addiction is devastating to a marriage, and I have met many couples who did not survive the impact. We decided that he would not be allowed to live in our home at least until he spent a considerable amount of time living in a sober-living group home where they would monitor his activities strictly while mandating attendance at meetings that address addiction. They would have rules on looking for and getting a job and they would drug test them regularly. We agreed that we did not have the inclination or the energy to be this twenty-five year old man's caregiver or gatekeeper. We need to survive! It is like when you are on an airplane and the flight attendant instructs you to put the oxygen mask on yourself before your child so you can both survive. Put the mask on the child first, then you pass out before you get yours on, and we'll see how long the child survives without you! It makes all the sense in the world, so why do we parents keep repeating the same enabling behavior and expecting a different result?

We have told Brandon that if he repeats his past behavior and relapses to drug use, that we are done with him and can not be his family anymore. Could we ever fully enforce our threat? Saying "never" is harsh language that rarely sticks. I said I'd never speak to my brother again ten times, but time marches on and things change. I have not spoken to my biological father in about fifteen years. We must enforce this even though the thought of having no relationship with our child is so painful that it is unimaginable. In all my years as a father, a coach, a mentor, I would never imagine that my child could be out of my life forever. If so, would it be easier? Or would the tidbits of information about his lifestyle if he relapsed be as painful as trying to help someone who can't or won't be helped because addiction has become everything to them. Addiction becomes their father, their mother, their brother or sister and their best friend all while it is simply their worst enemy.

Only the future will tell what happens with our Brandon. Will he be at our home, clean and sober as the new Brandon celebrating a holiday dinner with his family? It seems like an unlikely dream but it is all we desire. Will Brandon relapse and be on the streets as a gaunt resemblance of his potential self, avoiding the police until the inevitable arrest and incarceration or, God forbid, his death or complete disability from the ravages of years of drug abuse? Only time will tell what Brandon chooses and if his training and rehabilitation has given him the tools to survive.

Welcome Back, Time for You to Leave

Brandon returned to our hometown in December a few days before he was able to move into the sober-living home he had found. Most of the logistical work was in place and the residence was nearby. This meant Brandon would be home with us for three days, which would mean a few pretty tense days at the DeHaven household. He looked physically great but it was if he had landed on another planet. Brandon looked like a newborn foal trying to find his footing. He knew how he had disappointed us and the devastation to our family and he just looked at us like we might do anything from punch him in the nose to hug him. Brandon's younger brother Bryce was not about to tie a yellow ribbon around the old oak tree, a noose was a more likely greeting. Bryce was in fighting mode and had pretty much written Brandon off. Bryce's resentment towards Brandon was a physical and emotional stress. Bryce was so hurt by Brandon's relapse that he had ended up with severe stomach cramps, anxiety, and vomiting. Bryce had not dealt with the stress well, and it had landed him in the hospital several times—the stress was literally tearing him apart. Bryce put the blame squarely on Brandon and it was difficult to argue with his view. It was not likely that we could convince Bryce that this was not personal and that his brother was in fact suffering from a disease. Lisa and I needed to get Brandon into that sober living home ASAP before we had another broken nose!

The weekend finally arrived after three long days of a standoff between Brandon and Bryce. It really didn't matter how hard Brandon tried to be submissive and that he obviously was aware that he had caused this hatred by Bryce. It wasn't going to change until Brandon moved out, if at all, and that was all there was to it. Lisa and I were very impressed with how Brandon handled the constant combative attitude from Bryce. Again, I get it, Bryce is hurting and he is showing Brandon that he is in little brother's territory now, on his turf and Brandon is not welcome.

The repair of their relationship as brothers could take time, months, years, or possibly never happen at all.

Sober-Living

Walking into a sober-living home for the first time is a bit of a shocker. The place he chose with the assistance of the Narconon staff was a cluster of several homes with one main home all on the same block. My first thought was I'll bet the people that bought the home at the end of this block were less than delighted to have five consecutive homes filled dorm-room style with recovering drug addicts and alcoholics. When we walked into the entry we immediately felt the collective gaze of several dozen people surrounding a TV in a large common room. It was strikingly similiar to the large room at the Narconon center in Werner Springs where Brandon stood several years ago at his graduation of the rehab program. Stacking chairs were mixed among a variety of couches and chairs to accommodate those who were killing time in a common area. Off to the right you could see what looked like a very large food serving area but no food was out as it was past the scheduled dinner time of 5 p.m. A diverse crowd of people looked at us as if we had just wandered into a neighborhood bar, but in someone else's neighborhood! An odd silence joined the gaze as I had trouble finding the registration office. We obviously stood out as the parents who were dropping their son off at a sober-living home. A heavy man about my age stood up, lumbered towards us with a big-ninety percent toothless-grin and said, "Can I help you?"

"Where is the registration office?"

He pointed behind us, still smiling, as several others looked at us with a welcoming look, now seeming as if they might be trying to put us at ease.

We walked into the office and discovered a young man a little older than Brandon sitting well back in his chair with his shoes up on the desk. As soon as he saw us, he jumped to his feet and knew exactly who we were as we had an appointment. He was extremely pleasant as he pulled out a small stack of documents for Brandon to complete. It was as if we were buying a car or signing mortgage paperwork as he explained each page and showed us where Brandon needed to sign. Most of the documents covered the very stringent policies of staying at this facility. I asked the young man, "How long do people usually stay here?"

He replied, "It depends, sometimes one day and we have one person who has been living here since we opened, over twenty-five years ago!"

As Brandon signed the last page, we handed our credit card to the man to pay for his room which would include three meals a day available at very specific times. Just as we finished what appeared to be the last of the necessary documents, the gentleman looked directly at Brandon, held out a drug test kit and said, "Brandon, are you ready to pee for me?" Both Lisa and I were taken back by the bluntness of the question but Brandon obviously wasn't and he said, "Sure." The young man popped up from his seat and gestured Brandon towards an adjoining restroom. They both reappeared a few uncomfortable minutes later and the intake person said, "He's clean, so let's show him his room."

I can't tell you how much these simple words, "He's clean" mean to the parents of an addict— unless you already know.

We all walked back out into the common area and as we passed through all of the residents sitting around or gazing at the TV, they all got up and introduced themselves. Some offered to help if Brandon needed anything or some version of thoughtfulness. It was all so surreal that one minute we were strangers, and the next Brandon was a welcome resident and we were visitors about to depart this odd arrangement called a sober-living home. When you are the parent of an addict, you learn a lot about things that you had never before considered.

We visited Brandon occasionally, not spending much time inside the residence itself. We would either pick him up to grab a bite or usually walk across the street to a strip mall to buy him dinner and chat. It seemed like every time we came, he was in a different room with a different roommate or two or five! Honestly, Brandon seemed a little depressed over the living arrangements there but it could also be that he envisioned his own furnished and empty room at our house just a couple of miles down the road. I'm sure the thought of his own bathroom and some privacy was tugging at him, so near and yet so far as they say. His belongings were meager so moving from one room to the next wasn't a hassle as far as his personal items, but it was concerning to Lisa and me, and we could tell Brandon was getting uncomfortable in these surroundings as he was constantly on the go and constantly having to settle in with a new person or persons and the ever changing melting pot of occupants at this sober living home, referred to by those who lived there with the colorful nickname "Mad House," because of both its reputation and its location on Madison Avenue. I could tell he didn't like the constant change and although his rent included three meals a day, they ate breakfast very early, lunch at precisely noon and dinner at five on the dot. Not an unusual regimen considering the same existed at rehab, but in rehab they were awakened daily for training, counseling, and different study programs designed to prepare them for the outside world. Recovering addicts in this kind of living space are free to come and go as they please with the exception of a curfew and a mandate that they spend the night there unless they have an approved overnight leave of absence (LOA).

As I considered the strict rules, I wondered how that one person had managed to live there since Brandon was a toddler learning to walk. I guess it worked for that individual, and I speculated that perhaps that was the only way he could stay clean and sober in a life once consumed by addiction. Mad House also drug tested the residents randomly and always if they were late or broke a rule. Brandon would tell us that they lost people daily who tested dirty or just never came back in. What a job the management of this facility must have with several homes, ever changing occupants, feeding schedules and musical rooms to accommodate the revolving door!

Brandon was out looking for a job. I don't really know how a person does it when there is a three year gap in employment and an aversion to place a section in the resume noting, "Addicted to drugs, on the streets and off to rehab." The doors of opportunity that had been closed by Brandon so many years ago were very apparent every time he walked up to the door of a potential employer. Brandon would inevitably miss one or two of the scheduled meals a day while out on the job hunt, and if he did find a job, it would potentially conflict with his ability to catch meal time at Mad House. If Brandon thought ahead, he could request a bagged lunch be put aside for him, but Brandon was anything but prudent or organized after so many years of drug abuse. The food was not left out for snacking, it was promptly cleaned up after the designated mealtime and if you missed it, you got your food elsewhere or didn't eat. Rules are rules in the real world.

Living with the Addict in Remission

After about ten weeks, we all decided Brandon was ready to try living at home. (See Figure 7: Healthy Ways for a Parent to Support an Addict in Remission) He was more likely to find a job if he wasn't so restricted to times and hours. He hadn't really been able to eat there much while he was job hunting and so we told him he could live at home under the same rules as the sober living home with exception of hours. He had a strong job offer at a restaurant and his curfew at sober living would not allow the later shifts. And honestly, helping him by paying the rent there was starting to sting when we had an open room full of his bedroom furniture. We were very cautious as to not enable him, giving him all the yard work to do and many chores to earn his keep. He was extremely thankful and wonderful to have around as he was anxious to please us. He is so different when he is clean and a pleasure to be around. Included with his room and board was the requirement that he submit to a drug test any time I decided to administer it. Refusal to test equals dirty and that was a ticket out the door. The goal was to give him the ability to get a job, start paying off his many fines and bills and get him on his feet enough to move out on his own. Scary as it is, the little bird was going to need to fly—hopefully soar—through the air, and discover a wonderful life without drugs and not fall on his face.

A very typical situation with families grows out of the very realistic fear of losing the addicted child. What I've tried to say throughout this book is that if the child is addicted and his every move is compelled by his drug use, the child is already lost. We can all remember incidents in our life where our parents gave us tough love and although we were mortified at the time, we are now thankful that our parents were being tough and teaching us a life lesson.

Support: Support an addict in these healthy ways

Healthy Ways to Support an Addict in Remission		
drug test them like they did in rehab	don't give them money to go out	encourage them to dine with you
make them earn their keep if they're going to live with you	make them pay back their debt	surround them with family and invite them to family events
watch closely for signs of darkness and confront them on it	require them to attend meetings and verify their attendance	encourage open talks with sober friends in your family room
form relationships with the parents of their sober friends	find local support groups and attend them yourself	keep lines of communication open
watch for signs of relapse	support them in their job hunt	

Figure 7

There comes a time when the parents of addicts must release these children into the world. They will never find their bottom, their moment of epiphany, if they are locked in their bedroom with an endless supply of food in the fridge. This goes for a child who is actively feeding his addiction or one who is in remission. But if you, like we did, feel that really the best place for your child is home, they can't be there scot free. They have to be held to certain standards of behavior in order to live at home.

I am a big proponent of the written contract. Our son wrote one, with the help of his counselor at rehab. In his case, and I believe in many cases this would be true, the kid creates a plan for himself that would be tougher than one that you might create for him. But if it is necessary, the parent can certainly add to this plan, which becomes a contractual obligation for the child.

It seems like it might be a little late to have a realistic budget talk with your child, but looking at what they would pay for rent, utilities, food, transportation, etc. out on their own might help your child understand that life is good at home, and help them consider what they are willing to do to stay there. Tell the addict that you want them to write down under what conditions they will stay, and if they violate those conditions, they understand that they are no longer welcome in the house. One mandatory item on the list is drug testing and the failure of that test is a violation. Other items might be getting a job by a certain date, attending school, attending counseling, helping with specific chores around the house, etc. Have the addict sign the document and both of you keep a copy. A contract breach, including a dirty drug test, is grounds for expulsion.

I recommend providing a medium size piece of luggage at the time this contract is discussed. First attach the signed agreement to the luggage. Then, tell the addict that you would like them to pack that bag with essentials that they feel they would need if they were to move out on short notice. Place the luggage in the bedroom near the doorway so they get to walk past this constant reminder of their agreement. This agreement must be enforced, and this must and will look and feel different than any previous empty threats to "kick them out." This should be a civilized discussion.

I also suggest having the addict remove his bedroom door as a loss of a privilege of privacy and that bathroom doors are to remain unlocked or removed if the bathroom is inside the room. Almost every addict I talk to says they do the majority of drugs in the bathroom. Parents so often find that punishment is very difficult to enforce. So the threat of actually tossing out your child so they can hit their bottom is not as easy as a stranger or family member thinks. If that child dies on the streets, the parent will never forgive themselves or they may lose complete contact with this addicted child. The stress on a marriage is immeasurable, and the family unit is in turmoil. But, you know what, it's no better and less likely to change if you are part of the problem, doing too much, and not allowing your child to suffer the consequences of his actions.

Many years ago I was at a training event and they showed a recording of a man whom they had interviewed about the perils of not having health insurance. Now, I have been to more trainings, seminars and events than I could count. I have seen everything from novice speakers to several past United States Presidents speak, but the message from this man on a tape so long ago has stuck with me for all of these years, and I have passed on the abbreviated version of this man's advice. He spoke about his wife getting cancer and how the cost associated with her care had spiraled out of control to the point of bankrupting them. In the middle of all of this desperate care to save her life, the stress from the money and his wife's health issues combined had caused him to have a massive heart attack and hospitalized him, only adding additional financial and mental stress on their family. His wife died from the cancer as he lay in the same hospital fighting for his own life.

His basic analogy struck me as I quietly challenged the simplicity of his message in my own mind and the possibility that he could be correct. He said that only after all of this happened to him did he realize that "everything in his life could fit in one of his two hands." He held his hands toward the audience and he gestured his left hand higher than the other and announced this as "the hand I can do something about." He lowered that hand and raised his right, stating, "in this hand is the hand filled with the things in his life that I can do nothing about." He pushed this right hand closer and proclaimed that this is "the hand that will kill you!" He stated that his inability to make this simple distinction was his undoing and all the worrying and fretting about something that he could not control had caused him to have the heart attack and not be with his wife when she passed. The lack of insurance and the bankruptcy were already in motion and his obsession with things he could do nothing about would never change the inevitable.

He went on to say that he now knew that he should only focus on the hand which carried the things in his life that he had the ability to change or repair and that he would never again stare at the hand which held the things which he could do nothing about.

As I sat there reflecting, I found that he was correct and that there were things, problems and issues that hurt my life that I could not change and that my energy was better spent focusing on the things I could affect and change. You never give up immediately on anything, but you need to come to a conclusion at some point that no matter what you do, the inevitable will occur.

I thought about these two hands a lot during all the problems with Brandon and how his behavior was affecting my health, my wife's health, our marriage and our son Bryce in so many ways. This man who shared his wisdom with me and those words of wisdom that I had shared with so many others including my family throughout the years had caused me to think more about my behavior as an "enabler" to my son and his drug problem. Whenever Brandon fell, we caught him or picked him up and helped him because he was our son and we wanted him safe and healthy just as we had his whole life. Hell, I went undercover to bust known drug dealers and thugs to "help" (enable) Brandon so I was obviously willing to do literally anything to help my child. I think this is all a natural occurrence because you give birth to these babies, and then you care for them and keep them from harm the best you can and you just never know when or how to stop. Each child is so different and while one may wean themselves, the other may clamp on until they drown you or you make them sink or swim.

It was time for us to move Brandon to the hand that we could do nothing about. It wasn't going to be easy, and I guess it never is. But as they say, "Insanity is doing the same thing over and over again and expecting a different result." Just as nobody teaches you how to raise a child, nobody teaches you how to let go. Sure people make the simple statement, "Stop enabling" but it is easy advice from the backseat driver. It is up to the enabler to turn away and let them fall, and it does hurt when they do but what other choice do you have? Even though you know that it is likely the only thing that might stop the destructive behavior, we instinctively reach for our child when they fall.

It is important for the parents to find something to help themselves during this whole process. Different things work for different people. Personal therapy could work, as could group therapy. When we decided to find support meetings in an attempt to help us cope with feeling so alone, it wasn't hard to find Alanon meetings all around our area with a simple search of the internet. We attended Alanon meetings during our darkest times shortly after Brandon was busted, and we were strangers in a weird world of sad stories of addiction. We were such novices that we brought our son to our first meeting where we were the only one present with an addict. When it came time for us to introduce ourselves if we wanted to, I simply said, "We are Brad and Lisa and we are obviously newcomers to all this because we brought our addict with us," a collective chuckle put us at ease. Parents were present in droves with stories about bailing their children out of unthinkable predicaments (as if I have room to criticize). We were shocked to hear the age of these children who they enabled as being in their forties and fifties! When does it end? They never stop being our children, but we must find a way to give them the tough love of letting go when all else has proven to fail. They will never stand on their own two feet if you never let go!

Ultimately, we decided Alanon was not for us, and I was getting a therapeutic benefit from talking to other parents and writing. For me, writing *Defining Moments* was a catharsis, a working through, and writing was a process of discovery.

Forgiveness and Moving On

Before pushing the Publish button to send *Defining Moments* into the world, my editor asked me to sit down and read the whole book from cover to cover one more time. As I read, I cried softly at times or welled up in my office because I was reading about my life, and once I had put all the pieces together, it was sad and hurtful to relive but so cleansing to admit all of this to myself in writing. It hurt but it felt good to come to grips with so many dark moments and so many defining moments which had made me who I am today. I felt myself in every room and every situation as I read and I hoped that readers would feel as though they were sitting next to me as they read. I felt my natural deflection of nervousness in my humor and that was truly me. I honestly felt like my life was passing before my eyes and it was, in writing. My emotions were mounting and there were moments I could barely see through my welling eyes. A handful of tissues were clutched in my right hand as I continued to scroll down page after page. I gave instructions not to open my office door because, in all honesty, I was a mess. My heart pumped as I reached the end and read about Brandon's graduation ceremony as that was a day I will never forget and I again found myself hoping the reader would feel how I felt—sitting in that room full of unmatched furniture and healing souls all reaching for the brass ring of sobriety.

I reached the end and I read the last word, it was then that it hit me like a boulder crashing through my office window. I had forgiven Brandon, I understood that addiction was a disease, and worse yet, if I was forgiving Brandon, I must forgive all the addicts in my life! I had hated my biological father, my step-father, and my brother for so long. I hated them and now I had to forgive them if I was going to forgive my son.

What choice did I have? How could I forgive my biological father Richard for abandoning my mother and two young children and never even acknowledging our existence for so many years, not a dime of child support for my mother, left to fend for herself and care for two young boys when she was barely in her twenties?

How could I forgive my step-father Dino for beating me and torturing me as a child? For attempting and sometimes succeeding at making me feel worthless?

How could I forgive my brother for years and years of lies, deceit and verbal abuse and for how badly he continued to treat my mother, how much he destroyed her when she and I walked through the prison doors to visit him so many years before? How do I shed myself in an instant of something that was sewn into the very fiber of my being? Not only how can I but how do I forgive? What does it mean, what do I do? I was bawling in my office contemplating how and what to do to stop hating these people, these members of my family.

As I began to compose myself, I started to feel a calm, a clearness in my head and I didn't know this emotion that seemed to be a wave flowing through me. I realized that this feeling was forgiveness and that without making a call to literally state my forgiveness that I have just done it quietly in my room, by myself and with my thoughts. I forgive Brandon, Richard, Dino, and Thomas because I know that they are sick with an illness, a disease that can take many forms: addiction.

I never imagined that something this deep inside me and this profound and unhealthy could be released by my own will. How could something that had traveled with me for so long, something that defined me in so many ways be gone, lifted all in a moment? It seems so easy when I look back on it now but I knew as I sat in that office that hatred was torn from my body and it was replaced with peace and understanding. I was in control of hatred and forgiveness and oddly it was because I was willing and able to be brutally honest with myself in my writing. Reading my book was in fact a letter I did write and send to myself and the message I received was one of understanding and forgiveness. This was a priceless gift I had given to myself even if I didn't sell one book; I gained so much by writing it.

When I had my revelation that I must forgive all the addicts in my life, the first addict that came to mind was Thomas. As children, we had only each other and our mother and I wondered how substance abuse could erase all of that history, but that is exactly what it did. I had already forgiven Brandon and that in itself was how I came to the conclusion that the addicts in my life were all sick and therefore not truly responsible for their actions. I guess when a wife suddenly calls her husband every name in the book during childbirth, it is a natural reaction and they truly don't intend on hurting you. An addict's abusive words and actions can be difficult to forgive, and just because I had reached this point didn't mean the addicts in my life would be able to hear it. I then pictured forgiving Dino, but he had been dead for years. But I knew exactly where he was buried and it was a place I had not been in over thirty years. I could picture the graveyard and the tombstone but most of all, I realized that this was someone I could forgive, thank for what he did teach me (even if it was what not to do) and most importantly, he couldn't pick a fight in response, so that had a definite appeal to me.

I drove to the graveyard off Broadway in Sacramento and although this was not an area of town I frequented, I had driven past the cemetery several times over the years, but never down the street that lead to the entry and certainly never to the gravesite itself. As I turned down the street with the cemetery on my right, I watched the different shapes and sizes of tombstones and monuments to my right as I approached the entry gate. I actually find older cemeteries interesting and often time during our travels, Lisa and I will walk old cemeteries in historic areas like Boston, Richmond, and sometimes while exploring a country road we would stumble across a century old cemetery and take a walk through. Grave markers can be well over a hundred years old, and I am always surprised when I see fresh flowers next to a tombstone of someone who died over a hundred years ago. It makes me wonder who could still be paying respects, so many years later. Sometimes the flowers sit there and I can notice that the birthday of the deceased or the date of their passing was recent.

I drove through the gates and like a magnet was drawn along the curvy access roads directly to the spot of his grave like I had been there a thousand times before. It shocked me that I knew exactly where Dino was buried, and I gazed past a few tombstones between the road and the actual plot about twenty feet away. I got out of the car and walked towards his burial site and remembered the fiasco that was his funeral so many years before. There it was, unmistakable, Dino's tombstone with his picture mounted on the front, looking the same, frozen in time with that same painted on smile, he appeared to look directly at me as I approached. I knelt next to his grave and I told him that I forgave him for his abuse, that I knew now that he was sick and that it took my own child's addiction for me to come to grips with this feeling of hatred I carried for so many years. I know Dino was an alcoholic and I know that most of the time he beat me, he was drunk off his ass. I teared up a little as I thought of the dark moments in my life he represented but it felt good and right to me to be there and to say it out loud: "I forgive you." I wiped the tears with my thumb and rubbed my thumb across his picture so he could feel my tears. The picture of Dino began to shine as I passed my thumb back and forth over the picture. As expected he didn't say a word back; I think he took my message very well!

I knew then that the moment I had in my office when I forgave the addicts in my life was all I needed. I felt the release of hatred and I feel the healing from that moment even today. Every day the hatred gets further behind me. Like a bad relationship, it fades away and you think less and less about something that once consumed you. I still have dark moments just like everybody does when you let something get to you that should have never grabbed you like it did. I am a work in progress, but I do know that I unloaded a huge burden of hatred which I have carried for way too long when I decided to forgive the addicts who had so deeply defined me over my lifetime.

I also knew that nothing good was going to happen if I called Thomas or Richard and said "I forgive you." I didn't need to have Thomas or Richard over for a family dinner to make it all better. I didn't need them to acknowledge my forgiveness. I knew exactly how a conversation with Thomas or Richard would end and I knew it wouldn't help me heal. I just needed to forgive them in my heart and take my understanding of their illness and my newfound freedom from hatred and feel better within myself. No ceremony, no meeting, no nothing, just me forgiving them within myself was everything I needed.

I read about a woman who took the stand in a case where her family had been murdered by this deranged freak and she had been assaulted and she spoke during his sentencing to tell him that she forgave him. I know I was not alone wondering how she could ever forgive someone who had so viciously changed her life, but suddenly I understood the power of forgiveness. It was for her health that she forgave him. That is why I needed to just forgive the addicts in my life.

Figure 8

Resources:

Resources with More Information

The Parent Toolkit: parent.drugfree.org

Time to Talk: timetotalk.org

Parents: The Anti Drug: theantidrug.com

MADD: madd.org

Teen Truth: Drugs: teentruthlive.com

Five Moms Campaign: fivemoms.com

Parent Project: parentproject.com

Not My Kid: notmykid.org

Dose of Prevention: doseofprevention.com

Connect with Kids: connectwithkids.com

Smart Moves Smart Choices: smartmovessmartchoices.org

Conclusion

An addict is like an animal trapped in a cage. The cage that surrounds them is addiction, and some cling to that cage tighter than others. Some can be coaxed out into the sunshine and through the fog of addiction that clouds their mind, some will never release their grip or only release it through a lifeless body. You reach for them and they do not want your help, as they are snug in the corner attached to the back wall, as far from your grasp as possible. They will fight back at you much like a trapped animal who can't comprehend that you are here to help. You are seen as a threat, an obstacle in their course to continue feeding their addiction. They scratch, kick, bite, lie, lie more and tell you outright to leave them where they are, to forget about them forever. Through your frustration and outright exhaustion of trying to help someone who will listen to nothing you say and will not take your hand and follow you to help, you are exhausted, you are tempted to surrender; sometimes you do and sometimes you must so you can save yourself. The drug has them trapped. Their love for you seems gone forever because their addiction dictates their every thought and movement.

Sometimes you must push them away in an attempt to get

them back. You must let them hit their bottom, or see their light because you hit your bottom long ago and you have seen your light when you realize your help is enabling them. Your fear is that you will never see them again if you toss them to the streets so they can find their low and you may be correct, you may never see them again. You may blame yourself forever but what are you holding onto? You have a cage with an addicted child inside and it is not going to get better if you feed them, give them money or pay the rent. The fact is you are probably paying for more drugs! Addiction doesn't just get better one day. It doesn't just go away or keep its promise to be better or do less, and the longer you hold onto this cage the more embedded the addict becomes.

Addiction never ends well without professional help and even that is not a guarantee. As good as it will ever get is if you get an addict clean and in remission with an understanding of why they used, what triggers them and with the tools to just say no. With these tools your addict will come to realize that they don't want to go back to that life. The longer the remission the more likely you are to hug your child and watch them feel life drug free and hopefully find a future that is outside the cage of addiction. The journey through remission is moment by moment.

Give the cage to someone else to help free your child from addiction with the tools and the knowledge they need to live is this world. Letting go of your grasp of your addict may be the only way you can ever welcome back your child free of addiction. What Lisa and I have today, a healthy, happy son who is equipped to handle addiction if he chooses to, is the best you can hope for. He is an addict in remission, and every day I see his smiling face and wrap my arms around his healthy body is a blessing I will cherish forever, no matter how long it lasts. Brandon feels. And that is a giant step.

I am joined by so many wonderful caring and passionate people who also beat the drum of prescription drug reform, education and awareness; I am humbled by their dedication. Some march and gather others who are like-minded even though addiction has not decimated their family as they watch in horror as those around them suffer in this disease. Some continue to beat this drum though the heart in their child's chest beats no longer. Many wonder nightly as they have no idea what alley their child may sleep in or what hotel they sell their body in. The sound of a siren is a constant reminder of the unknown and thoughts of the worst scenario accompanied by hopes of a safe return. Few, like me, live with an addict in remission forever searching for signs of relapse. Many, too many, parents have lost their children to this epidemic and we understand exactly what a blessing it is to have our child alive at the end of the turmoil. So many parents wish they could wrap their hands around their child just one more time.

My goal and passion is to keep you from being in our club of suffering and worrying for the rest of your lives or standing over the grave of your child; to give you a better understanding that addiction can and does happen to ordinary people every day, no matter what you think you know and no matter how convinced you are that it will never be you. You are as mistaken as your invincible children that somehow you are exempt from a path that only gets darker and journey that only gets more impossible to return from.

Why is turning a blind eye to this epidemic so easy when the ramifications are so severe? Why would anyone ever risk asking themselves for the rest of their life what they could have done differently to alter the outcome of the lives shattered by addiction?

Please take this information to heart and know that I and others share our horrible stories so as to spare you from telling yours. Knowledge is the wisdom that can spare you the consequences of ignorance.

References

http://www.coalitionforplaceryouth.org/
<u>Addiction Medicine: Closing the Gap between Science and Practice</u>,
The National Center on Addiction and Substance Abuse at
Columbia University, June 2012
http://www.casacolumbia.org/upload/2012/20120626addictionmed.p
df
Behind Bars II: Substance Abuse and America's Prison Population